W9-AEJ-631

DATE DUE

Video Relay Service Interpreters

Studies in
Interpretation

Melanie Metzger and Earl Fleetwood, General Editors

Video Relay Service Interpreters

Intricacies of Sign Language Access

Jeremy L. Brunson

GALLAUDET UNIVERSITY PRESS

Washington, DC

Studies in Interpretation

A Series Edited by Melanie Metzger and Earl Fleetwood

Gallaudet University Press
Washington, DC 20002
http://gupress.gallaudet.edu

ISBN 1-56368-483-7; 978-1-56368-483-8
ISSN 1545-7613

∞ The paper used in this publication meets the minimum requirements of American National Standard for Information Sciences–Permanence of Paper for Printed Library Materials, ANSI Z39.48-1984.

Dedicated to Kelly Douglas Mease.
This book is as much a product
of my labor as it is yours.
Your love, passion, and support
are infused into every page.

Contents

Preface

What does it mean to be a professional? What is the appropriate relationship between a professional and a consumer? How does society's growing incorporation of technologies into everyday interactions complement and complicate these relations? It is these questions that are explored throughout this book. Before the reader begins, however, I think it would be helpful to understand the path that led me to take up these questions.

In 2001, I attended the business meeting that took place during the national conference of the Registry of Interpreters for the Deaf (RID). During the meeting, a motion was made that, if passed, would require any person wishing to test for a certification from RID to hold a college degree. Those in attendance were split on the issue. The argument put forth by those who made the motion and those who supported the motion was that a degree would, among other things, situate the field of sign language interpreting as a profession rather than an occupation. Unconvinced by the argument put forth by either side, RID referred the motion to a committee charged with exploring the issue further and making recommendations during the next conference in 2003, when it passed. While I was in support of the degree requirement, I was left wondering about its impact on the field and our consumers (see Brunson 2006).

A few years later, a service that had been around for some time began to be a staple in the field of sign language interpreting: video relay service. This new form of service delivery provided an opportunity for me to explore the issue of professionalization and sign language interpreting further. In the pages that follow, I lay out the findings of that project.

ACKNOWLEDGMENTS

The data discussed throughout this book were gathered for my dissertation. And although any errors are mine alone, it was the work of many people that made this project possible. The following people are those who have encouraged and inspired me, directly or indirectly, throughout this process. They asked about my work and progress. They told me that my work was important. And they patiently listened to me as I ranted about my work, sometimes incoherently, as I struggled to make sense of it all.

The first person is Professor Suzanne Vaughan. She introduced me to institutional ethnography and encouraged me to go to graduate school, an idea that had not entered my mind until she suggested it.

Of course, there is no way this document you are about to read would have been complete without my dear friend, guide, mentor, and dissertation advisor, Marjorie L. DeVault. She provided nurturing guidance throughout my training. She never told me what to do but helped me unpack the dialectics of every decision. I only hope that I am able to be half the scholar and mentor to others as she has been to me.

I cannot say enough about the participants of this study. They made this project possible. I will of course keep their confidence and only say you know who you are and I thank you from the deepest part of my being.

The next person is Jennifer A. Morse, a talented and gifted sign language interpreter and mentor. Although she probably never realized it, she made me want to understand the practice of interpreting as a process of negotiations. We spoke for many hours about how to improve our interpretations, and the end result was my realization that sign language interpreting is not a science, but an art. In the same vein, I acknowledge my Tuesday Night Family, with whom I spent several Tuesday nights rehashing the conundrums produced by various assignments; they gave me a language with which to talk about my work. I thank them.

I raise my hands and applaud the many deaf people who have accepted me into their world and taught me their language and culture, especially my dear friend, colleague, and language model, Gino Gouby, who has allowed me to bounce ideas off of him and has engaged me in insightful discussions about the relationship between deaf people and sign language interpreters.

Additionally, I acknowledge Deb Stone, who used her contacts in the Deaf community to make sure I had participants for my focus groups and who stayed late at work so that I could hold the focus group in her office. Without her help, chapter 3 would be incomplete.

I have to thank my family. While at times they may not have understood the project I was undertaking or the process involved to receive a doctorate, they provided me with encouraging words. My mother, Danette Brunson; my sister, Shawna Brunson; and my Aunt Robin have been tremendous.

My dear friends: Danielle, whom I met in graduate school, and who will always have a space in my heart, has demonstrated the meaning of fortitude, which inspired me, on more than one occasion, to continue my pursuits; and Emily, whose weekly lunch dates provided me with a reason to turn my computer off and take a much-needed break.

Any person who has embarked on a journey to create a dissertation realizes that her or his journey is often one of isolation. While gathering data, reading and understanding the literature through discussions with friends, and talking about the project with advisors and colleagues are extremely social acts, the actual writing of a dissertation can be a solitary practice. I, however, was fortunate enough to have my life partner, Kelly Douglas Mease, whose love for me allowed me to ramble about my work. He patiently listened as I told him of the exciting data I gathered, and pushed me when I thought I had bitten off more than I could chew. To him, and everyone who helped me along the way: Thank you!

Chapter 1

Toward a Sociology of Interpreting

Sign language interpreting is about access. The simplicity of the statement, however, belies the actual work that goes into producing, facilitating, and providing access. Access occurs through people's doings, both visible and invisible, both paid and unpaid. That is, access is the product of someone deciding to ask for an accommodation. It is the result of someone creating a line item for Communication Access Realtime Translation (CART) or an interpreter. Someone makes a call, someone schedules a service, someone makes a decision to accept or decline a particular assignment, and, if all goes well, someone shows up and provides access. The labor does not end there; more people must take up more work. Someone must accommodate the accommodation, by allowing the individual to set up and work in a place that lends itself to access. This can include allowing the interpreter to stand or sit in a place where the person needing the accommodation will be able to take advantage of it. And, of course, this does not include other invisible labor that goes into receiving an accommodation. While the interpreter is the one "providing" the access, making that access a reality is really the aggregate product of many people's efforts and doings.

CONCEPTUALIZING WORK BROADLY

Traditionally, *work* has had a limited definition. We have understood work to be an activity that occurs in a particular place, for a set duration, and under the direction of others. The focus is also on the stated function of the work in relation to the larger system in which it occurs (e.g., the relationship of customer service to the bottom line). Furthermore, work has been restricted to that for which a person receives remuneration. Feminist scholars and others have pushed for a broader definition of work (Daniels 1987; D. Smith 1990b; DeVault 1991). This new definition encompasses a wide range of activities that are both visible and invisible labor, essential to the operation of society, and those activities that are both paid and unpaid (e.g., mothering). Within this materialist view of work we can explore work as the product of people's activities, as well as the catalyst that drives people's activities.

Throughout this book, I use a Marxist-feminist understanding of work that recognizes both paid and unpaid work activities, focusing on the "labor processes" (Burawoy 1979), or the conscious, purposeful, learned activities that people perform with the intent that they will receive some benefit from them. These activities can include behaviors such as attending a company picnic in order to be seen as a team player, looking for a parking space close to the store to reduce the distance one has to walk, going through a drive-thru rather than cooking, or being nice to an interpreter coordinator in order to get called first for a job.

EMOTIONAL LABOR

One type of work is *emotion work*. "Emotional labor emphasizes the relational rather than the task-based aspect of work found primarily but not exclusively in the service economy" (Steinberg and Figart 1999, 9). Hochschild (1983), who introduced the concept of "emotion work," and others have examined the issue from the perspective of the service provider. More contemporary scholarship has attempted to further define and expand the meaning of "caring labor" (Himmelweit 1999). "Emotional work is performed through face-to-face or voice-to-voice contact" (Steinberg and Figart 1999, 10), just like all of sign language interpreting; therefore, we can discuss sign language interpreting as a form of emotional labor.

Most individuals who engage the public as a part of their job are more than likely participating in emotion work, but people also do emotion work outside of employment situations. For example, rather than focus on the emotion work between service providers and service receivers, Cahill and Eggelston (1994) study the emotional labor that individuals with disabilities—in their study, users of wheelchairs—perform to spare themselves and "walkers" any awkward feelings. Schwartz (2006, 112) finds that deaf people as well engage in emotion work, a phenomenon he calls "letting it go": For example, deaf people allow doctors to end appointments before answering all of their questions, because they sense the doctors getting impatient.

One form of emotional labor is care work. Himmelweit (1999) suggests that the definition of "care [work] should be reserved for relationships in which the recipients are dependents who cannot provide for their own needs, though more broadly it could be extended to include reciprocal relationships of true equality" (30). England and Folbre (1999) define care work more broadly: "Care work includes any occupation in which the worker provides a service to someone with whom he or she is in personal (usually face-to-face) contact" (40). Although England and Folbre do allow for the possibility that other kinds of interaction (e.g., writing) could also be considered care work, they focus on face-to-face interactions.

I suggest that sign language interpreters and the people with whom they work, specifically deaf people but non-deaf people as well, have a reciprocal relationship. Interpreters often learn at least some American Sign Language (ASL) from deaf people. The work that interpreters perform depends greatly on the relationship that develops between the interpreters and the deaf and non-deaf persons they are working with. Furthermore, deaf people's access does, at times, depend on the sign language interpreter's mood; as I discuss in chapter 4, interpreters who feel they have been disrespected by the deaf (or non-deaf) person may choose to withhold services until they receive the respect they feel they deserve. Therefore, deaf people must engage interpreters with the understanding that their relationship is one of reciprocation. They must teach would-be interpreters ASL and, in some cases, acquiesce to the interpreter's demands in order to get access through them. In these ways the work of interpreting can be classified as care work and examined through this lens.

As some scholars have discussed (see Baynton 1996; Branson and Miller 2002; Davis 1995, 2002; Lane 1999), deaf people have rejected the label *disabled*. Therefore, conceptualizing the interaction between interpreters and deaf people as care work is political. The connotation is that someone needs to be taken care of, which may reinforce some of the stereotypes about people with disabilities, such as the idea that they are "more dependent, childlike, passive, sensitive, and miserable and are less competent than people who do not have disabilities" (Linton 1998, 25).

I introduce the idea of care work despite this concern because I believe that we should disrupt the negative connotations associated with asking, needing, and receiving care. There are very few (if any) people in the world who can sustain the claim that they have gone through life without benefiting from someone's care work. This care work can be overt, such as the service of a caretaker (e.g., parent or partner) or paid service provider, or it can be more covert, such as the emotional labor done to spare a person's feelings. I feel that both types of care work should be embraced as necessary components of a civil society.

ACCESS

Rejecting the disability label, most deaf people prefer instead to be considered a linguistic minority. "Deaf advocates such as Paddy Ladd, Tom Humphries, and MJ Bienvenu claim they have nothing in common with amputees, paraplegics, or people with mental retardation" (Davis 2002, 37). Rather than accept disability as an inherent condition of the individual, some deaf people point the finger outward to explain the ways in which the world is not accessible to them by design; they see society's audism as the problem, not their deafness (Lane 1999; Davis 1995; Baynton 1996; Branson and Miller 2002). This is exactly the argument put forth by Disability Studies scholars. Disability Studies scholars, in examining disability as a social construct, have looked at the ways in which people with disabilities have been systematically excluded from society. An outgrowth of this exclusion is a need for access.

Whether one is negotiating one's car onto the freeway or entering a building, gaining access requires work. However, for certain populations, gaining access is not as simple as deciding to enter a building. For those, such as deaf people, who rely on others to gain access, a forced collaboration occurs. Both deaf people and interpreters must do their parts to create access. History has shown that access can be achieved in two ways. The first way requires a radical shift in the everyday practices of the populace, to include an outright acceptance of difference. The second way, not as dramatic a change, requires society to make accommodations.

We can look to Martha's Vineyard from the seventeenth century to the early part of the twentieth century to see how outright acceptance of difference can lead to access. In *Everybody Here Spoke Sign Language: Hereditary Deafness on Martha's Vineyard,* Nora Groce (1995) documents the societal acceptance of deafness among the people of the isolated community of Martha's Vineyard between 1600 and 1900. Not every person on Martha's Vineyard was deaf, but there were unusually large numbers of deaf people, most likely a result of inbreeding. Most people on the island, deaf and not, used sign language to communicate, even when speaking with people who were not deaf. Within this accessible environment, deaf people were able to hold positions in local government and participate in the daily life of the island.

As Groce talked with people who had lived on Martha's Vineyard, she discovered that there was often uncertainty as to who was deaf. People were known not by their differences but by their contributions to the community. Groce points out that "the Martha's Vineyard experience suggests strongly that the concept of a handicap is an arbitrary social category" (108). Furthermore, "the most important lesson to be learned from Martha's Vineyard is that disabled people can be full and useful members of a community if the community makes an effort to include them" (108).

THE FIELD OF SIGN LANGUAGE INTERPRETING

More commonly, people who are deaf or hard of hearing gain access to the larger society through the use of an intermediary. This intermediary can take several forms. In some cases it can be a simple pen and paper or typing apparatus. In other situations, a more sophisticated means is necessary, such as a person who is trained in two or more languages and who understands two or more cultures—a sign language interpreter.

As long as there have been deaf people, and non-deaf people with whom they need to communicate (except in rare communities such as Martha's Vineyard), there have been interpreters to bridge the communication gap between people who rely on a sign language to communicate and those who do not. The field of professional sign language interpreting, however, is relatively young. It was not until the establishment of the Registry of Interpreters for the Deaf (RID) in 1964 that payment for the services provided by interpreters became the norm. Prior to this time, most interpreters were volunteers and do-gooders (Neumann Solow 2000) who typically held full-time employment in other fields and provided occasional interpretation services for friends and family members (Fant 1990).

Sign language interpreting has now blossomed into an employment niche in which interpreters can sustain themselves and their families on the income gained from interpreting. They have a national organization, RID, that tests and certifies interpreters, lobbies on their behalf, and maintains a registry of practitioners in the United States, Puerto Rico, and parts of Canada.[1] RID has worked to define the practice of sign language interpreting as a skill-based trade that requires extensive training. In a few states interpreters and deaf people have lobbied successfully for requirements that interpreters hold one or more RID certifications in order to charge for interpreting services.

CONVERSATIONS ABOUT PROFESSIONAL STATUS

The term *professional* has come to mean a person who performs a certain task for money, for example, a professional football player. A football player who is a professional does not necessarily have special theoretical knowledge; "professional" conveys only that he receives money to perform. Furthermore, professional does not refer to the ranking of a particular occupation in relation to another occupation (i.e., a cook versus a chef). To determine whether someone is a professional, some focus on relations in which someone engages. Marianne, an interpreter educator and interpreter referral owner, says:

> I want to be perceived as a professional and I think that we are being held back because of others. [. . .] Because that is how I perceive myself. That is how I want to be perceived. That is what I want to project. [Being a professional] means a couple of things. It means respect to the consumer, the deaf person, and respect to me. Value for the money [we earn]. We get paid a lot. [. . .] I consider it a profession because that is how I want it to be. That is where I see it going, where it should be. Interpreting is rather new . . . but I think we should walk the walk. We can't wait until others see us as professionals before we behave like professionals. We need to lead by example. Show people how it should be.

For Marianne, being a professional means one behaves in a particular manner. She wants to be "perceived" as a professional but implies that one can be a professional without such recognition.

Sociologists take a much broader view of what it means to be a professional; indeed, there is a wealth of sociological literature relating to

---

1. Canada has another organization, the Association of Visual Language Interpreters of Canada, that serves the same purpose as the Registry of Interpreters for the Deaf in the United States.

the study of the professions. Rather than looking solely at the individual, sociologists look at the ways in which individuals are part of a larger social structure that situates some individuals as professionals. In society, labor that is invisible or unpaid is often seen as less valuable than labor for which people are paid. This value is often associated with the prestige of a particular occupation. In the United States, for example, secretaries are given less prestige than CEOs; police officers have more value than groundskeepers. The value of occupations is increased when society sees them as professions rather than merely occupations. Sign language interpreters have been trying to gain recognition as a profession; it was toward this aim, in an attempt to reconceptualize interpreting as something other than "charity" (Fant 1990), that practitioners vying for professional status formed RID.

Professions are different from occupations in that professions "are *deliberately* granted autonomy, including the exclusive right to determine who can legitimately do its work and how the work should be done" (Freidson 1970). Five characteristics distinguish a profession from an occupation (see Carr-Saunders 1928, 1988; Greenwood 1957, 1988; Hughes 1960): a systematic body of theory, professional authority, sanction of the community, regulative code of ethics, and a professional culture. In the "trait approach" to understanding professions (MacDonald 1995), scholars examine how many of the five characteristics a particular occupation possesses. The trait approach can help chart the development of a profession: By the number of professional characteristics a particular occupation possesses, one can place that occupation on its path of development into a profession.

Power of a Profession

It can be useful to examine traits possessed by a particular occupational group, but there are some limitations. Namely, a focus on particular traits does not provide us with an understanding of the power dynamics between professionals and those who use their services. Although those in attendance at the 2001 RID Conference did not openly discuss the idea of power that is afforded to a profession, it was present. That is, there is an assumption that any occupation that is recognized as a profession will enjoy certain freedoms. Hence, part of the definition of profession is the power professionals wield.

Eliot Freidson is a scholar whose work illustrates an examination of the power of professionals. He has written a number of books and articles on the place and powers of the professional in society. In *Professional Powers: A Study of the Institutionalization of Formal Knowledge*, Freidson (1986) describes the professionalization process and the authority professionals are able to wield in society. As other scholars have done, he suggests that professionals hold a significant and influential role. He refers to this power as "professional autonomy," or the ability to exercise control over one's work. And this prestigious position in society is in part due to the acquisition of an advanced education.

Professional autonomy goes further than mere control over the immediate work, however. Once professional status is achieved, this autonomy brings with it the power for practitioners to act as gatekeepers. As gatekeepers, professionals are able to determine the criteria that must be met in order for someone to join the profession. They also protect their own professional "turf" or jurisdiction. For example, in the field of nursing (Wertz and Wertz 1997; Reverby 1997), as physicians achieved professional status, there was a change in the types of procedures nurses and midwives could perform. Particular procedures were reserved for physicians, and persons who were not licensed physicians could face sanctions if they performed them.

Occupations that have achieved professional status have *functional autonomy* (Freidson 1970, 1986; Conrad and Schneider 1997). Practitioners who have functional autonomy are afforded the ability to determine how to best go about performing their work. However, "the autonomy connected with skill should not be confused, as it often is in the literature [and by sign language interpreters], with the economic autonomy of the traditional self-employed professional" (Freidson 1994, 73). Once in a profession, a person's practices are evaluated by the standards established by the field (e.g., codes of conduct). These standards are not always known or understood by lay persons and therefore it may seem a person's decisions are beyond reproach from those outside the field.

However, the very status that allows professionals to be evaluated by their peers is also part of a system of control over that professional's work. Recognized professions, such as physician, are heavily regulated by the state. Although physicians have significant functional autonomy as they interact with individual patients, there is also a great deal of oversight from the state and from insurance companies.

In addition to functional autonomy, professional status brings with it the authority to define a given situation. It is this claiming ownership over a particular phenomenon that situates the professional in a position of power over those for whom she provides services (Spector and Kitsuse 2001; Gusfield 1989). Just as with work, often scholars have focused on the function of a profession rather than exploring what Abbott (1988) calls the *ecology* of a profession. That is, very little attention is given to the relations that the professional maintains with clients and other professionals.

Professional Identity

Some scholars, such as Hughes (1971), rather than count traits or talk about the power afforded to professionals, prefer instead to understand the meaning attached to being a professional. Hughes ties the meaning to the prestige of the label. The move, or labeling, of an occupation to a profession comes about by occupational mobility, of which there are two kinds.

The first type of occupational mobility is individual. The individual works to increase his knowledge and hopes to use that knowledge to secure his position in the social hierarchy. The other way is by group mobility. Hughes (1971) suggests that as society is quickly changing, people within particular occupations are unable to quickly adjust; therefore, people of particular occupations, rather than learn additional skills or change occupations, work to change the status of their occupation by renaming it a profession. This can include the practice of limiting who enters a particular field through tests, education, and association fees. One example of this is the medical field; doctors enjoyed very little prestige in the United States until the Jacksonian period, when they began to redefine who could become a physician (Conrad and Schneider 1997; Starr 1982).

However, the status of a professional field is not fixed. Scholars have also written about the processes of *deprofessionalization* and *proletariatization* (Pandey 1988). If occupations can become professions through the specification of particular traits or characteristics, then the opposite would hold true. Just as occupations can achieve professional status, they can lose it. The authority that professionals possess is in part due to their control of knowledge. As more people have access to that same body of knowledge, one might expect that the professional's authority wanes. However, Freidson disagrees with the deprofessionalization and proletariatization theses, stating:

Threats to the professions' monopoly over defined bodies of complex knowledge and skill stem from a number of sources. Insofar as their formal knowledge can be stored in a computer, it loses its esoteric character because anyone can retrieve it. The computer, furthermore, can be used to assess professional performance according to the authoritative standards stored within it. Another threat to the professions' monopoly over specialized knowledge stems from the lay population's increasing levels of education, which makes people less inclined to see this knowledge as mysterious and more likely to be critical and challenging in their dealings with professionals. (Freidson 1994, 131)

Freidson contends that although more people are becoming formally educated, that knowledge, for the most part, is too general to usurp professional authority. Furthermore, for those individuals who have gained specific knowledge, we must recognize that specialization has also occurred and that professional specialization would work against deprofessionalization through the loss of knowledge. However, Freidson is referring to the field of medicine. Practitioners in the field of medicine have already gained professional status; sign language interpreters have not.

Both the trait approach and the functional autonomy approach take a removed, categorical approach to examining the professions. To examine the work of professionals and the impact of their relations with people who use their service, I prefer to use a materialist approach. Materialism allows us to explore the actual processes involved with defining one's work as professional. Beginning in the actual doings of those who wish to achieve professional status will help explicate the linkages between the individual and the structures. To begin on the structural level, aside from being premature, would mask the struggles that occur as a result of this change.

I submit that attaining professional status, regardless of the field, changes the dynamics between the practitioners and those who procure the services, as well as among the practitioners. Positioning practitioners of sign language interpreting as superior in knowledge about deafness to deaf people is not the only quandary that faces the field of interpreting. The advent of video relay services within the last few years has added another dimension to the organization of the work that needs to be explored vis-à-vis the deprofessionalization and proletariatization processes. Video relay interpreting services allow deaf people greater ease in communicating via the phone through the use of a sign language interpreter. However, interpreters are employed by the video relay service provider and hence bound to the regulations established by the provider, much like physicians and their relationships with insurance companies.

Video relay service regulations from the Federal Communications Commission (FCC) and particular video relay service providers encourage interpreters to standardize their practice. Interpreters' judgments are replaced by rules, policies, and computer programs. That is, video relay service is designed so that interpreters rely on computers, rather than their own needs or those of their clients, to dictate when they take breaks, accept a call, and transfer a call. This is all in the name of efficiency (DeVault 2007). Whether this dependency on technology is evidence of the "proletariatization" (Pandey 1988) of the field of sign language interpreting, or simply a reorganization of professional work (Freidson 1986), remains unclear.

Employment and Salary of Sign Language Interpreters

Practitioners of sign language interpreting are a group that deaf people must engage nearly every day as they interact with nonsigning individuals. Many interpreters have friends, family members, or loved ones who are deaf. They have received at least part of their training in American Sign Language (ASL) from deaf people through deaf functions. Many interpreters who do not have deafness in their family can recount stories about going to Deaf Bowling Night with deaf people. Others spent a lot of time at the Deaf club when they first started learning sign language. It was there that they were taken under the wing of deaf people and taught the language and culture.

Deaf people's goals are usually different from those of a student wishing to become an interpreter. Deaf people are helping someone learn their language so that they can one day have an interpreter who is fluent in ASL. The students, on the other hand, while hoping to become fluent in ASL, are also hoping to one day make a living interpreting. Therefore, there is the possibility that the same people who took the fledgling interpreters under their wing and shared their language and culture will one day have to go without an interpreter because they cannot afford to pay the fees of their one-time mentees. With a few exceptions, most settings interpreters find themselves working in are controlled by non-deaf people. In business meetings and legal, medical, and educational settings the interpreter is working in her second language, most of the time interpreting from English to ASL. In some situations, deaf people are allowed and encouraged to participate, but their participation is often limited. When they do participate, it is often with short answers and in response to the prompts of non-deaf people.

Although there are occasions when interpreters provide services in-kind or pro bono, often, interpreters are paid for their services. Interpreters work as both staff interpreters and independent contractors. Organizations that have a high demand for interpreting services, such as educational institutions, service agencies for deaf people, and state and federal offices offer staff positions to interpreters. Along with a salary, staff positions offer benefits associated with full-time employment. Although the primary duty of staff interpreters is to provide interpreting services, interpreters are often responsible for other duties when they are not interpreting.

Independent contractors, on the other hand, are responsible for providing their own benefits and are not obligated to perform any task other than interpreting. The national standard maintains that independent contractors charge a two-hour minimum for all interpreting assignments. Prior to video relay service, an interpreter who held a certification from RID could earn between $30 and $35 per hour for interpreting jobs that were not considered to be legal in nature. Legal assignments were usually charged at a rate between $35 and $50 per hour. After video relay service centers were established in multiple cities, the rate in those areas began to increase to compete. In 2007, one video relay service provider paid interpreters between $34 and $38 per hour. Another service provider recently began paying interpreters $46, plus a bonus of up to $5 per hour for achieving the recommended call-processing time. It is now not uncommon for interpreters to earn between $40 and $50 for nonlegal assignments.

Models of Interpreting

When the field of sign language interpreting began to formalize in the mid-1960s there was little understanding of the complexities of what interpreters do. Before the practice of interpreting received the attention of researchers, different philosophies emerged to shape how interpreting work should be carried out. Four main philosophies emerged, each of which marks a changing understanding of interpreting work.

HELPER PHILOSOPHY

In the early years of the field, interpreters were not formally trained practitioners but were talented friends, neighbors, and family members who accepted the responsibility of interpreting for the deaf people they knew and loved. This philosophical approach situated deaf people as "handicapped, limited, and unable to fully manage their personal and business affairs" (Humphrey and Alcorn 1994, 202). Practitioners working under this philosophy often assumed responsibility for managing deaf people's lives; interpreters commonly conducted all of the business for the deaf person and told the deaf person what had happened only after the interaction was over.

CONDUIT OR MACHINE PHILOSOPHY

The machine philosophy developed as a response to the helper philosophy. Under this philosophy, the empowerment pendulum swung to the other side of the spectrum. Practitioners behaved, as the name suggests, like machines. In extreme cases, interpreters would make no cultural adjustments while interpreting between languages. Therefore, sentences were spoken as they were signed and would often sound like broken English, making the deaf person sound unintelligent. In less extreme situations, the interpreter would pretend to be invisible, taking on the role of a telephone. The interpreter would merely transmit the message without consideration of culture or context.

BILINGUAL/BICULTURAL PHILOSOPHY

Recognizing that the conduit or machine philosophy was not producing effective interpretations, leaders in the field developed a new approach. They decided on an approach that encouraged practitioners to show respect and appreciation for the linguistic and cultural components of a given interaction. In the bi-bi philosophy, as it is called, the emphasis is on getting to know the deaf persons for whom they are interpreting. This philosophy also calls for an understanding that interpreters are dealing with two separate languages and cultures and that both are important; ideally, this allows practitioners to provide a more accurate interpretation, promoting communication access for both the deaf and non-deaf persons equally.

ALLY PHILOSOPHY

As a branch of the bi-bi philosophy, Baker-Shenk (1991) began a discussion of a new philosophy. This new philosophy situates interpreters not as cultural mediators, which is how interpreters often see and talk about themselves under the bi-bi philosophy, but as allies to the deaf people with whom they work. That is, under the ally philosophy practitioners are encouraged to recognize the power that it is inherent in their work. Interpreters are also called on to appreciate that deaf people have long been oppressed; if they took as their mission only to provide communication access, they would be culpable in the further oppression of deaf people. Instead, Baker-Shenk argues, interpreters should work to benefit the deaf person. An argument against this model is that this philosophy suggests that interpreters should not be neutral in their work, which already impossible (Metzger 1999).

Interpreters can be seen alternating among the philosophies depending on the setting and the demands it places on the interpreter. For example, when interpreting for a woman in a delivery room, the interpreter does not merely interpret but is more likely to employ the philosophy associated with the helper, holding legs, providing comfort, and calling for nurses and doctors when asked. Similarly, there are times when adopting more of a conduit persona is ideal. When interpreting for deaf people who use their own voices or who are embarrassed about using an interpreter, the interpreter is more likely to attempt to blend into the setting and work to provide interpreting visuals of the auditory message. As I will discuss, interpreters in this study also employ various models of interpreting. Some of the interpreters I spoke with chose a particular model as a means of retaliation against a deaf person they considered to be rude, whereas others simply preferred one model over another.

Although there are times when interpreters employ different philosophies, most interpreters typically favor one philosophy. An interpreter's choice of philosophy often depends greatly on where and when the interpreter was trained, as well as on whether the interpreter has kept up with the literature within the field. Interpreters trained in the 1970s may favor a conduit or helper philosophy, whereas those trained in the 1980s and 1990s are more likely to favor the bi-bi and ally philosophies. These interpreters, who believe in bridging communication between people by taking both cultures and languages into consideration, feel they can best achieve this by getting to know the people for whom they are interpreting. Bi-bi- and ally-approach interpreters must never forget that as interpreters they wield a great deal of power and that deaf people have experienced a lot of oppression in society.

Each of the philosophies developed as practitioners gained a better understanding of the intricacies of their work. In exploring the organization of signed language interpreters in video relay service, we can see the ways in which this organization restricts interpreters' autonomy to use their professional discretion in determining which philosophy is best suited for a particular situation. Rather than allowing interpreters to employ the philosophy they deem appropriate, video relay service mandates impose a conduit philosophy practice. And, in doing so, they diminish interpreters' ability to provide accurate and message equivalent interpretations (Weisenberg 2007).

DEAF PEOPLE AND THE TELEPHONE

It is misleading to talk about deaf people as if they are a homogenous group. Deaf people vary in their range of hearing, communication styles, politics, views of deafness, and a whole host of other issues. Some deaf people have been deaf since birth (prelingual deaf), while others become deaf later in life (postlingual deaf or late-deafened).[2] Those who become deaf later in life may choose not to learn to use any form of sign language. These individuals typically socialize with non-deaf people and are likely to identify as hearing impaired or hard of hearing.

As stated earlier, deaf people's communication varies. Of the various communication modes that deaf people use, ASL is the only naturally evolving language. When placed on a continuum, ASL would be placed on one side and on the other side would be English-based sign systems.

ASL is the dominant language used by people who are deaf in the United States and parts of Canada (Baker-Shenk and Cokely 1980). ASL is not a form of English. It has its own grammar and syntax that are represented with hand shapes and movements, or signs. "Individual signs are themselves structured grammatical units, which are placed in slots within sentences according to grammatical rules" (Padden and Humphries 1988, 7). Deaf people can express both abstract and concrete ideas using ASL.

Those people who were born deaf or became deaf before they were able to speak are more likely to use sign language and interact with others who use sign language. People in this group share beliefs and values about what it means to be deaf. Here, *deaf* does not mean the lack of hearing; it is not viewed through a pathological/medical lens. Rather, it

2. Oliver Sacks's 1990 book, *Seeing Voices: A Journey into the Deaf World,* provides further discussion of prelingual and postlingual deaf individuals.

signifies membership in a group in which the members express themselves visually using (in the United States) ASL and attend residential schools for the deaf. It also denotes the struggle for a world that is not based on sound. Although video relay service can be used by either group, use of sign language is required.

Deaf Community

Being an effective interpreter requires, in part, understanding communication variation within the population with which one works. Deaf people's communication styles vary greatly. Kannapell's (1982) typology of communication styles of deaf people is useful in understanding the range and diversity within the Deaf community: Kannapell suggests that some individuals are only comfortable communicating in ASL; others are only comfortable communicating in an English-based signing system; and still others fall along the continuum in between these two extremes. Individuals falling at these two extreme positions are referred to as *monolinguals,* while those individuals who fall at other places on the continuum are referred to as *bilinguals* and *semilinguals,* to denote their fluency in both expressing and understanding both ASL and English. Through continued interaction with members of the Deaf community, sign language interpreters are able to see the range of communication styles on which Kannapell's typology is based and are better equipped to interpret into and from these communication styles.

ASL is a visual language that does not have a written form (although W. C. Stokoe and Valerie Sutton did attempt to create one; see Hoemann 1986). A written form of ASL would have to be extremely intricate to include the nuances of a three-dimensional language; thus, no attempts have been successful over the long term. Without a written form, the language must be transmitted from one generation (or person) to the next through face-to-face communication. As such, there needs to be a "good rapport between speaker and listener" (Padden and Humphries 1988, 3); this is another reason why interacting with members of the Deaf community is an essential practice in the field of sign language interpreting.

Often, there is not a verbatim translation from ASL to English. This is why the first attempt at providing telephonic access for deaf people—the text relay service—was not completely effective; communicating in a written form meant that deaf people were using their second (sometimes third or even fourth) language. Individuals whom Kannapell (1989) referred to as "ASL monolinguals" (23) struggled with text relay service, whereas those who had some skill in English fared much better.

Individuals who identify as a member of a linguistic minority and embrace their deafness as a cultural marker make up the Deaf community. When distinguishing, in writing, between people who see their deafness as a pathology and those who view it as a cultural marker, it is customary to use d*eaf* and *Deaf*, respectively (Padden and Humphries 1988, 2005; Baynton 1996; Lane 1999). When referring to both Deaf and deaf people without regard to culture, it is customary to use the term *deaf people*.

It is tempting to assume that interpreting for a deaf person is the same as interpreting for a Deaf person. However, this is incorrect. The only difference between deaf people and the people they are conversing with on the phone is modality. Therefore, there are very few adjustments an interpreter must make. Interpreting for Deaf people, however, requires interpreters to possess the linguistic abilities and also the cultural awareness and savvy to mediate across cultures (Cokely 2001). The culture of deaf people is what anthropologists would consider "high context" (Hall 1976). That is to say, communication among deaf people is based on shared (or learned) experiences. There is a focus on in-group relationships. Members of the in-group are defined as those who share political, linguistic, social, and audiological perspectives (Baker-Shenk and Cokely 1980).

Although people can possess one or a combination of these characteristics, only those who possess all of them (e.g., deaf people) are considered members of the Deaf community. Other people may interact, work with, or get raised by deaf people, but their membership in the Deaf community is only honorary.

Due to the high-context culture of the Deaf community, it is mutually advantageous that interpreters befriend deaf people. By doing so, interpreters are able to learn the language and culture of deaf people while improving their receptive and expressive skills in ASL. As with all communication, there is a lot of implicit meaning behind comments. Interpreters who do not interact or otherwise maintain familiarity with the culture of deaf people quickly find that they are unable to interpret effectively. "It is imperative that interpreters keep up with new coinages as well as alterations in usage of the languages in which they interpret" (Stewart, Schein, and Cartwright 1998, 129). The benefits to deaf people of interpreters' continued involvement with them is that they are able to get to know who their potential interpreters are and provide them with the necessary skills in ASL and deaf culture to be effective interpreters.

In recent years, a new system enabling telephone access for deaf people has emerged: video relay service (VRS). Using broadband technologies, video equipment, and sign language interpreters, deaf people can place calls to anywhere in the world using ASL, their first language. During my career as a sign language interpreter, I worked for three different VRS providers, in five centers located in four states.[3] This book focuses on data that I collected while working for one provider, Ease Communication, Inc., and explores the organization of work of sign language interpreters who are employed by the VRS industry. Although my data for this book came from one provider, I and many of my colleagues have worked for multiple providers; in our conversations it became clear that as interpreters leave one provider and join another, they take ideas with them. Therefore, many of the practices of video relay interpreting are similar, not only because interpreters work for multiple providers, but also because the regulations placed on providers are the same.

LEGISLATING ACCESS

In 1980, Paul C. Higgins wrote, "[Deaf people] are outsiders in a world largely created and controlled by those who hear. The deaf live within a world which is not of their own making, but one which they must continually confront" (22). The world is still created and controlled by those who can hear, and deaf people are still forced to contend with it. However, since 1990, there has been legislation in place that aims to promote access for people with disabilities: the Americans with Disabilities Act (ADA), which some say would not have passed had it not been for deaf people (Shapiro 1993).

In 1990, George H. W. Bush signed the ADA into law. As an inclusive piece of legislation, the ADA provides people with disabilities protection against discrimination in a variety of venues, and it was heralded as a monumental piece of legislation that furthered the rights of people with a range of disabilities (National Center for Law and Deafness 1992). The framers of the legislation outlined four broad categories under which persons with disabilities might experience discrimination: employment

---

3. My methodology is located in Appendix A.

(Title I); access to state and local government and public transportation (Title II); public accommodations (Title III); and telecommunications (Title IV). Miscellaneous Provisions (Title V) is a supplement to the previous four titles.

Title IV is most deeply implicated in the organization of the work of sign language interpreters who work in VRS centers to provide telephone access between deaf or hard of hearing and nonsigning individuals. Under Title IV, telephone companies are charged with providing services to deaf people that are "functionally equivalent" to those services that people without hearing loss enjoy. This mandate has been interpreted by the FCC as requiring telecommunication services for the deaf in the form of text relay or video relay services. However, the ADA does not provide guidance on what is meant by "functionally equivalent"; therefore, providers are also responsible for defining this objective and putting into practice measurable steps that will meet it. This is a key component of accountability (McCoy 1998). In VRS, "functionally equivalent" is a number in a report rather than effective interpretation. Behaviors that can be seen and tallied, such as logging in and out of the system, the amount of time spent on each call, and how long each caller has to wait in the queue, are some of the measurements of whether a deaf caller's experience with VRS is functionally equivalent to that enjoyed by non-deaf people with the telephone. However, this type of calculation does not take into account whether the interpreter is able to interpret from English into sign language that the deaf caller understands, whether the interpreter speaks in grammatically correct English while interpreting from ASL to English, or whether clear communication between the two callers even occurs. This calculation of functional equivalency actually hides the work of deaf people as they attempt to take advantage of this service and the work of interpreters as they work to provide accurate interpretations.

THE EVOLUTION OF TELEPHONE SERVICES FOR DEAF PEOPLE

Not-for-profit organizations established for and by deaf people had been experimenting with ways to make the telephone accessible for deaf and hard of hearing people prior to the passage of the ADA. For example, in 1987, at the insistence of the California Association of the Deaf (CAD) and the Greater Los Angeles Association of the Deaf (GLAD), the utilities commission made available to deaf and hard of hearing persons the ability to place a call, through a typist, to another person who was not deaf or hard of hearing (Padden and Humphries 2005). After the ADA's mandate, various phone companies around the United States instituted telecommunication relay services (TRS).[4] These services, funded by a phone tax paid by all citizens who have a phone, allow people who are deaf, hard of hearing, or speech impaired to place calls through the aid of a third party, known as a communication assistant, and a teletypewriter for the deaf (TTY).[5] The call can be initiated either by the person with a speech or hearing impairment or by someone without such impairment.

Deaf people and the telephone in fact have a long, intertwined history. After all, Alexander Graham Bell's mother had a hearing loss and his wife was deaf (Winefield 1999); some suggest that Bell developed the phone in an attempt to help his wife hear. Some scholars have compared sign language interpreters' work to that of a telephone. Sharon Neumann Solow (1981) writes:

> The sign language interpreter acts as a communication link between people, serving only in that capacity. An analogy is in the use of a telephone—the telephone is a link between two people that does not exert a personal influence on either. It does, however, influence the ease of communication and the speed of that process. If the interpreter can strive to maintain that parallel positive function without losing vital human attributes, then the interpreter renders a professional service. (ix)

Ironically, the telephone has been one of the areas of social life that deaf people have been unable to take advantage of on an equal footing with their non-deaf counterparts. And while some have blamed the telephone and other technologies for the demise of the deaf clubs (see Padden and Humphries 2005), some deaf people have considered the telephone a symbol of oppression, referring to the denial of telephone access a form of "communication violence" (Jankowski 1997). Regardless of on which side of the aisle a person is situated, deaf people are now guaranteed telephone access through Title IV of the ADA, which requires "all telephone companies to provide intra- and inter-state relay services across the United States" (Center for Law and Deafness 1992, 205).

---

4. Telecommunication relay services (TRS) were the standard for relay. With the advent of video relay, TRS has come to mean "traditional" relay service, as opposed to VRS.

5. This is sometimes called a telecommunication device for the Deaf or TDD.

FIGURE 1.1. *TTY relay system. Source: www.fcc.gov, retrieved July 12, 2007.*

The first relay system relied on a non-deaf person, known as a communication assistant (CA), who uses a headset or traditional handset to hear what the non-deaf person says and then types it on a teletype machine or TTY that the deaf person then reads; the deaf caller then types a response for the CA to read back to the non-deaf person. All three individuals are in different locations. To initiate the relay call in the United States, 711 connects a caller to a CA, who can be located anywhere in the country. At the time it was established, this system was considered to provide "functional equivalency" on the telephone for deaf persons (see figure 1.1).

As technology improved, broadband technologies enhanced telephone services for deaf people. New technology uses broadband, video cameras, and individuals trained in providing sign language interpretation between deaf people who sign and nonsigning individuals to provide video relay services, which are considered to be more "functionally equivalent" telephone services for deaf people. In VRS, an interpreter working in a call-center environment sits in a cubicle in front of a camera. A large (32-inch) television, a computer, is connected through an earpiece to a telephone, and places calls to and from deaf and non-deaf people. Once both the caller and the person being called are on the phone, the interpreter, who is seen by and able to see the deaf person, provides a sign language interpretation of the spoken language (English or Spanish), and vice versa.

This new service replaces the CA with a sign language interpreter who is still able to hear the non-deaf person using a headset, but, rather than the interpreter having to relay messages by reading and typing, the interpreter and deaf person see one another on a television screen and communicate with each other in sign language (see figure 1.2).

 shows: Video relay user signs to the interpreter (1), Interpreter speaks to the phone user (2), Phone user responds (3), Interpreter signs the response (4).

FIGURE 1.2. *Video relay system. Source: www.fcc.gov, retrieved September 15, 2007.*

In allowing deaf people to communicate in ASL through a sign language interpreter over the phone, VRS takes an idea from a staunch oralist, Alexander Graham Bell (Winefield 1999), and allows deaf people to use their native language, ASL, to communicate with people around the globe.

Video Relay Service versus Video Remote Interpreting

Before continuing, it is important to delineate between two seemingly similar services that have been categorized differently by the FCC. Both VRS and video remote interpreting (VRI) use broadband technologies, sign language interpreters, and video equipment to provide communication access to people who are deaf or hard of hearing. However, they differ in how they are regulated and paid for. With VRS, none of the individuals can be in the same location. That is, for the service provider to be reimbursed for the provision of the service by the FCC, the deaf person, the interpreter, and the nonsigning person must be in separate locations. In situations using VRI, two of the people, typically the nonsigning and the deaf person, are in the same room. This is common when, for example, a deaf person is in a remote or rural area where there are very few, if any, qualified interpreters and it would be cost-prohibitive to send an interpreter from a nearby city to interpret for the deaf person and her physician, for example. The FCC does not reimburse for this service. The service provider and the hiring entity have a service contract. Video relay service, not video relay interpreting, is the focus of this book.

Getting a Videophone

There are multiple VRS providers in the United States. Some of them have manufactured their own videophones whereas others use the technology of their competitors. Some of these providers give deaf people a videophone (camera), free of charge, that can be used to make VRS calls; others charge a fee for their equipment.

Organizations can also get videophones. Agencies that serve deaf and hard of hearing people, companies with deaf or hard of hearing employees, and schools for deaf children are also typically equipped with videophones. On the campus of Gallaudet University, the only liberal arts college for deaf and hard of hearing students in the United States, one video relay service provider has placed several videophones in the cafeteria and other locations. Similarly, on the campus of the National Technical Institute for the Deaf, which houses programs for deaf, hard of hearing, and non-deaf students, it is not uncommon to see several videophone stations installed by one VRS provider.

Initially, some providers required that all calls made on their videophones go through interpreters that they employed. This allowed for them to recoup the cost of the manufacturing through billable minutes. A deaf person without multiple videophones from various providers, however, was limited to only one provider regardless of her satisfaction with the service she received.

In 2006, after being petitioned by several video relay providers, the FCC made a Declaratory Ruling that stated that requiring deaf people to have multiple videophones or limiting their ability to use multiple providers was "inconsistent with the notion of functional equivalency,"[6] and required that all video relay service providers make their videophones interoperable. This ruling makes it possible for deaf people to have a videophone from one provider but use it with any provider they choose.

THE APPROACH AND ORGANIZATION OF THE BOOK

This book is not intended as a critique of VRS, of interpreters who work for VRS, or of the deaf people who use the service. Rather, the purpose of this book is to demonstrate the ways in which this service is

---

6. DOC-265218A1[1]

organized and to illustrate how that organization influences, for better or worse, the actions of people who engage it. I am not attempting to generalize the experience of the various people I interviewed, worked with, and observed to that of all deaf people or all those who work in VRS. That is not my goal. My goal is to demonstrate the larger organizing mechanisms.

Institutional ethnography provides a method for exploring the social that begins in the everyday activities of people's lives. Although Canadian sociologist Dorothy E. Smith is credited with developing it as a method of inquiry, institutional ethnography has been taken up by scholars in various fields to examine a wide array of issues. Scholars have employed institutional ethnography in the exploration of the state's attempt to regulate sexuality (G. Smith 1988; Kinsman 1995); it has been used to uncover the practices that attempt to remove discretionary judgment from the work of nurses (Rankin and Campbell 2006); and it has been used to document the ways in which the work of nursing home attendants is organized to focus more on the production of paperwork than on human interaction (Diamond 1992). The commonality among all institutional ethnographies is that they are the tools of activists; the end result is a "map," or understanding, of how things are put together that can be taken up by people and used to effect change.

The term *institution* in the approach does not refer to a physical location in which people are housed. Dorothy Smith uses the term to indicate a "functional complex such as education, health care, and law, in which several forms of organization are interwoven" (Grahame 1998, 352). There are three main tasks involved in producing an institutional ethnography. One is to unpack the ideological practices that make the institution's processes measurable. Another is to recognize the work, in the broadest sense of the word (e.g., not just paid work), that people perform in the creation and maintenance of their everyday/everynight worlds. The third task is to identify the ways in which the localized everyday/everynight practices are linked to extralocal sites (D. Smith 1987). Institutional ethnographers typically begin in their everyday/everynight worlds and are inspired by a disjuncture they encounter there.

DISJUNCTURE

My disjuncture occurred when I first began providing interpreting in VRS for Ease Communication nearly four years ago. I was informed of various rules I had to follow while I provided *access* to deaf people. These rules, some of which have changed over the years, dictated how interpreters are to interact with the callers. The first rule prohibited me from conversing with the deaf caller prior to or during the call. When the deaf person appeared on my television screen, with the exception of verifying the phone number they wanted to call, I was not to engage the caller. This included a prohibition on providing the deaf caller with my actual name; instead, I was only allowed to give them a number. The second rule focused on what information could be interpreted; if the deaf person stepped out of the screen or was looking for something to write with, I was told not to provide an auditory description of what I was seeing. I was not to interpret the visual cues.

These seemingly arbitrary policies were counter to my training and my practice of providing sign language interpreting. Although I initially attempted to adhere to these rules, I soon found myself "violating" them to enhance my interpretation. Although I did not openly converse with deaf callers, I did, when the deaf person came up on my screen, ask clarifying questions. For example, I would ask whom they were calling. I would ask, "Do you want to talk to someone specific? What is his name?"[7] This typically would result in the deaf caller explaining who they were calling and the purpose of the call. This information helped me with the context of the call I was about to interpret.

In regards to the rule about not interpreting visual cues, I eventually disregarded it completely. For example, when a deaf person left the screen to grab a pen, I would say, "Hold on for a second while I grab a pen." If, while talking with her bank, a woman began to fumble through papers on her desk, I might say, "Now where did I put that statement?" Even though the caller did not say, in sign language, that she was going to get a pen or needed to find her bank statement, my understanding of phone etiquette, non-deaf people's uneasiness with silence, and my previous experience attempting to avoid interpreting visual cues—which often led to confusion and communication breakdown—taught me that saying nothing was detrimental.

As I talked with other interpreters whom I respected, I found that they too were disregarding these policies. The collective justification was that Ease Communication had hired professional interpreters and interpreters

7. Although these questions are written in English the actual modality was sign language.

should not only be able, but be encouraged, to exercise their judgment. It was obvious to us that the corporate understanding of interpreting was based on a misunderstanding that sign language interpreting is a science; whereas I knew from experience as a practitioner, trainer, educator, and occasional consumer that there is a lot of artistic license involved too. I felt that Ease Communication had failed to recognize the actual work of interpreters. This work is not solely a matter of choosing a sign for a word or even a phrase to convey a concept, but rather one that includes negotiating relationships between people.

Since I had been reading the work of Dorothy Smith and other institutional ethnographers I began to see these policies as not merely shaping my work but also connecting my labor to someone else's labor. I saw them as someone else's product; because I had to read and adhere to (or contest) these policies, I was connected to the person(s) who created them. I began to see Ease Communication as part of a larger, translocal organizational complex. That is, the company could be seen (and examined) as the nexus of the work of various people occurring in various places. This inspired me to explicate the complex coordination of VRS.

My Problematic

A problematic is not merely the "troublesome, perplexing, difficult, etc." (Grahame 1998, 348), but a "complex of concerns, issues, and questions which generate a horizon of possible investigations" (348). As such, I take up as my problematic the changing nature of the work of sign language interpreters, which is influenced by the burgeoning applications of broadband technologies. I aim to understand how and by whom the work of sign language interpreters gets organized and how that organization redefines relationships between service providers and service users. To explore this problematic, I start in the everyday/everynight lives of interpreters. I work to understand from the empirical world, not the theoretical (see Blumer 1954).

The Product

All work has a product. That is, there is something produced from people engaging in a particular activity. In regard to VRS, the product of the labor of the various people involved is a phone call—successful or otherwise. The following is a transcription of a phone message left for a video production company. The call was placed from a deaf caller using

VRS. Names and other identifying markers have been removed to protect the identity of the caller, interpreter, and the production company.

Hi . . . Hi Joe . . . Hi Danielle Keith. . . .

I'm calling because I wanted know . . . about the videophone and the process . . .

(long pause)

. . . the powering, the cabling . . . for the tech services . . . um, we applied . . . for that loan last Monday. . . . and we have some money for that project . . . the deaf and the hard of hearing raised the money . . . for the ASL and the deaf club . . . and, ah, so the people here from Nebraska wanted to know what the process is to develop that . . . you know, is the need rising or is it declining? And we have several interested members, different age categories. Umm, this message is rather long I know . . . so I wanted to know if ummm . . . you can take care of these or answer these questions for me.

I know we have a total of about seven thousand five hundred dollars. Hmmm . . . so hopefully you won't exceed that any cost that is needed.

Ummm . . . we can go ahead and use this from July of 2006 to July of 2007. . . . and of course I'd like to do some of the presentations at uh . . . at uh . . . the . . . any of the campuses that would require me . . . um, or would ask for my services. And again, we have different age categories, different organizations that have raised this money.

Um, we can also maybe incorporate some videotapes . . . with this money . . . You know, something pertaining to ADA law . . . ummm, you know, senior citizens involvement. So, um . . . again I know this is a rather lengthy message but if you have some please email me, OK? Danielle Keith? My number . . . dkeith2@hotmail.com . . . and of course you can also contact me at the videophone. I was going to give you that number but you should have it. Alright? Um, so I hope everything works out and you can answer my questions. Thank you.

This message was left by Interpreter 3560.

It should be noted that I do not know whether or not this particular interpreter worked for Ease Communication. Furthermore, it is not possible for me to know the credentials of this interpreter or if this was the last call of a long, busy day. All I know is that this was the message left by a deaf person on a non-deaf person's answering machine and that the goal, presumably, was to discuss an issue that at least one person felt was important enough to warrant a phone call.

The person who retrieved this message was unable to decipher the purpose of the call. How is it that a call, using the latest technology, intended to provide access, can fall short? One explanation is that the interpreter lacked the ability to perform the requirements of the job. Others may say that the deaf person was sloppy or too fast and therefore the communication breakdown is the deaf person's fault. And still others might look at the video relay provider and argue that the various policies they have established make it impossible for interpreters to do their jobs effectively.

I suggest that this call, and many others like it, are products of the coordinated organization of the work of interpreters along with the others involved in the interaction. There is an organizational complex that includes and extends beyond deaf persons as consumers, interpreters as practitioners, and VRS centers as service providers that operate in an attempt to produce access. This organizational complex is tied to the global economy, conceptions of disability, the practices of invisible and emotional work, and the desired trajectory of the field as a whole.

Throughout this book, I examine the work that deaf people and interpreters do in an effort to receive and provide access. I illustrate the way that this work is being reorganized as part of the "new managerialism" (Rankin and Campbell 2006), which focuses on percentages and other numbers rather than effective interpreting. Each chapter moves the reader further from people's actual doings and into the extralocal regulatory agencies. My analysis of these regulatory processes will demonstrate, much like Campbell's (2008) study on the continuity of care, how a practice that aims at fostering communication access based on each individual's needs is replaced by efficiencies embedded in texts.

In the pages that follow, I introduce readers to various actors and their roles in the provision of VRS. It is my hope that as these actors and their roles come into focus, an illustration of the way in which sign language interpreting services are part of a larger institution (D. Smith 2006), one that I call the "institution of access," will become clear.

In chapter 2, readers will become acclimated to the environment of VRS. In this chapter, the focus is on the architecture of the locations in which VRS takes place. I provide the general layout of the two centers I studied and discuss the ways in which that layout and the organization of work in the centers change the practice of interpreting.

In chapter 3, the focus shifts to deaf people who have used video relay service. This chapter provides insight into the experience of the intended users of this service. Again, the focus is not on the generalizability of the participants' experiences; it is an examination of the generalizing effect of the organization of those experiences.

In chapter 4, practitioners talk about their experience working in VRS and how it differs from working in face-to-face interactions. Chapter 5 takes up the texts that interpreters encounter in their work and explores where they originate and how they are used.

In the final chapter, I lay out the implications of this organization of the work of VRS interpreters on the field of sign language interpreting as a whole. I also discuss the potential impact of this book on the scholarship of sign language interpreting.

Chapter 2

The Architecture of Access

Video relay service centers are the nexus at which various people's work of creating access meet and become tangible. The *architecture* of the video relay centers is a broad term that refers not only to physical structures, but also the organization of activity within these spaces. The physical structure of the call center houses multiple people and pieces of equipment, and it creates a defined space. In doing so, the architecture also organizes the relations that occur in that space. People who enter this defined space physically or virtually have specific roles and titles. Whether they are client, employee (contract or staff), manager, or custodian, their behavior is organized by the space they are in and the title they have in that space. In addition to highlighting the organizing effects of the layout and work processes of the center, this chapter gives readers who are unfamiliar with VRS a glimpse into a center.

Years before VRS became a reality I attended an interpreter training program. A talented interpreter came to one of my classes and talked about her work as an interpreter. She opened her presentation by saying "We interpret everything from birth to death." That statement stuck with me throughout my training, and since. I have been called on to interpret business meetings, promotions, terminations, loan applications, doctor's appointments, the birth of children, the burial of loved ones, depositions, criminal trials, and a whole host of other interactions in which deaf people find themselves having to deal with non-deaf, nonsigning people. The advent of VRS has made it possible for my colleagues and me to enter into yet another realm of deaf people's lives that interpreters have not often been privy to on a consistent basis: telephone interactions.

People, as social creatures, are constantly devising ways in which we can maintain connections to one another. Using various mechanical devices, people are able to stay "in touch" with people across the street or across the globe. The telephone represents one such way. It is used to connect people to friends and family, to place orders for everything from foods and gifts to services and clothing. Although the passage of the Telecommunication Enhancement Act of 1986 enabled deaf people to have text relay services that enabled them to use the phone (National Center for Law and Deafness 1992), through VRS, deaf people can now stay in touch with friends and family and order goods and services using their first language, ASL. They are able to enjoy the benefits their non-deaf counterparts have enjoyed since the telephone first appeared in U.S. homes in the early part of the 1900s.

Telephone service, and the human connections it encourages, is also a business. The success of that business depends on the ability of the technologies to perform effectively. Businesses spend a great deal of money to ensure that the technology, environments that house the technology and the operators who interface with it operate correctly. To do otherwise would be bad business.

Although I have and draw on my experience as a sign language interpreter working in five different VRS centers, the data I discuss are primarily based on participant observations I conducted at two VRS centers for one particular provider, Ease Communication.

THE PHYSICAL ENVIRONMENT

The call centers are in locked office buildings that require access cards to enter. On the multiple occasions I did not have my access card, I had to ring the doorbell and wait for another interpreter to let me in. Of course, an auditory doorbell would be distracting to interpreters and callers so the centers have visual alarms—slow flashing strobe lights—to alert people that someone is "ringing" the doorbell. There are also deaf staff members in the centers. These visual doorbells also allow them to know someone is at the door.

The centers I worked in have cubicles in rows. Each interpreter sits in a cubicle that has a 32-inch television, a complete computer, with Internet access, and a videophone. In addition to the hardware in the cubicle, each station, as they are called, has various documents. These documents include the protocol for processing different types of calls (e.g., local or international) and for transferring calls, training information, and scripts that are to be read aloud to the non-deaf person or signed to the deaf caller. Although the location and manner in which these various texts are displayed differ (one center had them in a binder while the other one had them pinned to the cubicle wall), the information is the same type.

These protocols are located in a place that makes them easily accessible to the interpreters but out of sight of the deaf callers. This does not mean that deaf people are unaware that these documents exist. In fact, on many occasions when a deaf person asked for the number to technical support, I hurriedly looked around my cubicle trying to find the number. Undoubtedly, they were able to see me looking around. I also would, at times, open up the binder to the correct page, in front of the camera, and sign the number to the caller while reading it off the document. But to have too many papers in the background of the interpreter could be distracting to callers.

These documents provide quick resources for a variety of technical issues that could arise for signed language interpreters. Another reason for these documents is to standardize practices. The goal is to cover a range of scenarios in order to limit the amount of individual discretion each interpreter must exercise. By increasing standardization, VRS providers aim to make interpreters interchangeable and thereby allow Ease Communication to use interpreters to fill a time slot rather than a communication need. That is, the primary goal is to have enough interpreters to cover the expected call volume. Whether or not the interpreter is the right interpreter for the particular call is a secondary consideration.

Figure 2.1 is a sketch of one of the VRS centers I worked in. The environment has typical office equipment. A facsimile machine, a copy machine, and a printer are all available for us to use. In addition to the office equipment both centers also have a break room. (One center I worked in after I completed my research does not have a break room. It only has a large table in the middle of the room where interpreters congregate to eat and chat.) The break rooms are different in size and setup and in the items provided. I was told that it was up to the center manager to decide what items to stock in the break room. For example, in one center there is a variety of snacks. The other one simply has bite-sized candy (e.g., M&Ms and Jolly Ranchers). One of the centers has a soda machine from which interpreters can purchase drinks for $1.50; the other has only a water dispenser. The larger of the two has two couches where interpreters can (and do) sleep during their breaks. The other one has a paraffin wax hand bath that interpreters can use to soak their hands in at the end of their shift to help with aches and pains related to repetitive strain injury,[8]

---

8. Repetitive strain injury can "result in carpal tunnel syndrome, tendonitis, tennis elbow, and brachial neuralgia" (Humphrey and Alcorn 1994, 183).

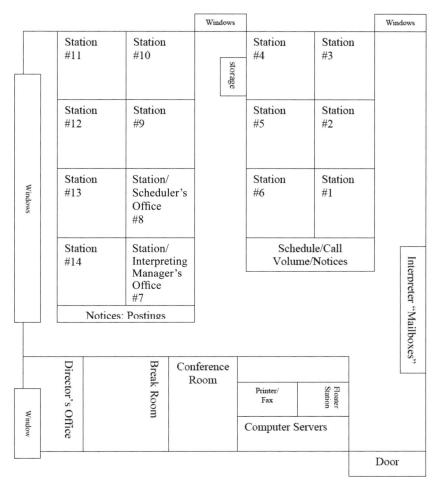

FIGURE 2.1. *Ease Communication, Inc., Relay Interpreting Services Center: Southwest site.*

which can end an interpreter's career prematurely. Both centers have sinks and notices about safety and the federal minimum wage on the walls.

Outside the cubicles, the walls of the centers are adorned with information about schedules, events, trainings, certification test dates and locations, interpreting-related news (e.g., conferences), and praise. Both centers have an entire wall devoted to certificates of appreciation for different interpreters. Some interpreters have multiple certificates from deaf callers. To receive these certificates, either caller (deaf or non-deaf) must send an email or call customer service and report their appreciation for the interpreter's work. (I will return to these certificates in chapter 5, where I will discuss their uses and their relation to other texts used to monitor interpreters' work.) In one of the centers, there is another wall that congratulates newly certified interpreters or interpreters who received another certification from RID.

In VRS centers that are regulated by the FCC, call confidentiality is a consideration. And, although the call centers are laid out in rows, they differ from traditional "call centers [that] are of necessity open-plan, with each team's workstations grouped into cluster or row formation" (Baldry et al. 2006, 239). In traditional call centers, such as those that Baldry et al. (2006) discuss, the open plan allows for supervisors to observe several employees at one time. In contrast, each wall of the cubicles in these VRS centers is six feet high. The design is intended to prevent eavesdropping by those who pass by the cubicle and by those interpreters who are working nearby, to protect the privacy of the callers.

VRS centers are also designed to create productive workers. Another function of the six-foot walls is that interpreters are not likely to become distracted by things outside the cubicle. If the walls were lower, interpreters could look over and see other deaf people who were making calls. Furthermore, there is the potential for a deaf caller to see other deaf people if the walls were too low. Due to the height of the walls, the only way to see into the cubicles is through the door-size opening used to enter and exit the cubicles.

Since the walls are high, there are lights on top of the walls to alert others that there is a call being interpreted. When assistance is needed, interpreters can either send a message to all interpreters using the Instant Messaging program or, because of the close proximity, they can simply ask for assistance from a nearby interpreter who is not interpreting a call at that moment.

Two- and Three-Tier Centers

Ease Communication categorizes its centers by its layers of management. Whether a center is considered a two-tier compared to a three-tier center has little impact on the daily work of the interpreters, but there is a certain level of prestige, at least for management, associated with a three-tier structure. When I first heard about the tier classification, I assumed that three-tier structured centers could handle more calls than did two-tier structured centers. I was incorrect. In fact, the two-tier center I worked in, housing twenty-four stations, is much larger than the three-tier center, which has only fourteen stations. In the two-tier centers, the administration consists of the scheduler and the manager; a three-tier center also has a director.

CAST OF ACTORS

Each center is filled with various people who perform different functions. Depending on the size and location of the center, the hierarchal structure of the center and the number of roles within that hierarchy may differ somewhat.

Sign Language Interpreters

In VRS centers, a sign language interpreter is called a video interpreter (VI). Each center has a number of interpreters working at any given time. Some interpreters prefer only to work days, Monday through Friday, while others prefer only to work at night, depending on the interpreter's other responsibilities (i.e., families, school, and other paid work).

There are three classifications of VIs at Ease Communication That is, VIs are either on staff at Ease Communication or work for the center on a contract basis. A VI who does not hold a national certification from RID is considered to be an "interpreter-in-training." Interpreters-in-training are staff employees, but their continued employment is contingent on them taking and passing RID's national certification examination within a given time frame, typically six months to a year. However, some interpreters-in-training unable to pass the RID exam or to get a testing slot because there are not enough spaces available are terminated. Interpreters-in-training provide an inexpensive source of labor for Ease Communication because noncertified interpreters are paid less than certified interpreters, but they can still accept calls that the center bills to the FCC.

STAFF INTERPRETERS

Interpreters who choose to become employees of Ease Communication, like I did, are required to fill out an application, provide information for a background/credit check, and submit to a urine test to detect potential drug use. Staff interpreters may have additional responsibilities in addition to interpreting calls. These responsibilities can include creating a newsletter, helping out with reports, sitting on committees for birthday parties (i.e., getting cakes and cards), morale improvement, and other non-interpreting-related activities.

In one center, all of the staff interpreters are also assigned chores, typically focused on cleaning the break room, to complete during their shifts. There is a list of duties and interpreters assigned to each affixed to the break room door. The interpreters place their initials next to their name to indicate the task was completed. I did not experience or witness any consequences when interpreters did not complete the duties they were assigned. Regardless of their additional functions, their primary role is to provide sign language interpretation for callers.

Staff interpreters can be classified as either part-time or full-time employees. Their status depends on the number of hours per week they work. Typically, part-time employees are not allowed to work beyond 29 hours a week. When I asked about this rule, Belinda, the manager for one of the centers, told me, "Working an average of 32 hours a week in a quarter constitutes full-time employment. Therefore, 29 hours gives us some wiggle room. Also, this allows interpreters to work more in one week if the call volume is high." Although the rule is 29 hours, and this turns out to be the average in a given quarter, when the call volume is high, centers lift the cap on the number of hours an interpreter can work.

Full-time employees are scheduled for 40 hours per week, but they are only on the phones (e.g., interpreting calls) for 32 hours. The other 8 hours are spent assisting with administrative tasks and taking care of other, noninterpreting tasks.

FREELANCE INTERPRETERS

Similar to staff interpreters, the primary function of freelance interpreters or independent contractors is to interpret calls. However, unlike staff interpreters, freelance interpreters are only responsible for interpreting. Although they may, and some do, participate in committee work, many of the freelance interpreters I spoke with only provided interpreting services.

Freelance interpreters also have a different application process. Freelance interpreters must satisfy the Internal Revenue Service's definition of an independent contractor. One manager pointed out a manual provided by the federal government that aids companies so that they can ensure that their contractors are indeed contractors according to the IRS's policies. To accomplish this, the interpreters must provide an invoice with their own letterhead and their tax-identification number. Furthermore, they must provide a statement that they do and will continue to work for other agencies.

Requiring freelance interpreters to provide additional documentation protects Ease Communication from workman's compensation claims. Without this additional documentation, interpreters who were unable to continue to work due to repetitive motion injuries or carpal tunnel syndrome, a common occurrence among interpreters, could claim that their injuries were the result of working at Ease Communication and file a worker's compensation claim against the center.

Not only do freelance interpreters have limited responsibilities, at Ease Communication they are also paid differently and not provided benefits. Because taxes are not paid on the employee's behalf, the additional documentation provides proof to the IRS that the interpreter, not Ease Communication, is responsible for their employment taxes, which include the federal income tax withholding, Social Security and Medicare taxes, and the federal unemployment tax.

Just as part-time staff interpreters are limited to a maximum number of hours they can work in a week, so are freelance interpreters. Freelance interpreters are not permitted to work beyond 29 hours per week. Because part-time employees and freelance interpreters are not able to get benefits, they are typically paid based on their certifications and experience alone. Therefore, it is not unusual to find part-time employees who earn just as much per hour as a freelance interpreter.

INTERPRETERS-IN-TRAINING

In an effort to increase the pool of interpreters, Ease Communication instituted a program for training would-be interpreters.[9] These interpreters are theoretically within six months of gaining a national certification from RID. Often they have very little experience in any arena and thus bring very little practical experience to video relay.

Ease Communication provides these interpreter hopefuls with training and guidance as they study for, and eventually pass, the national exam. This training often includes sitting with certified interpreters, meeting weekly with a trainer to discuss situations and prepare for their certification examination, and attending workshops. Training that takes place while sitting with certified interpreters depends on the certified interpreter's

9. One video relay provider has also started an "institute" for training interpreters. Although this might increase the number of interpreters for video relay service, it also further stretches the already thin resources of interpreter trainers (see Brunson 2010).

style. In my case, I allowed interpreters-in-training to watch me interpret a few calls, then I would ask if they were ready and willing to take some calls with me by their side. After each call, regardless of which of us was interpreting, we would take a few minutes to talk about the pros and cons of the choices we made while interpreting. I have spoken with other interpreters who never let interpreters-in-training take calls and those who immediately put them on the phones and took breaks. The idea is that interpreters-in-training, as long as they are in training, will work alongside a certified interpreter so they are able to receive helpful feedback. However, it is not uncommon to see these interpreters working alone taking calls just a few weeks after starting and prior to earning certification.

In some cases, interpreters-in-training are allowed to work without a certified interpreter immediately even though they have not received the full training. At times, this is the subject of great discussion among certified interpreters because interpreters-in-training are being scheduled for hours that could go to the certified interpreters. When I asked a trainer about this, he said, "I was told that it is very costly to have the [training program]. We are paying these people but they are not processing calls. That means that we are losing money." Some interpreters-in-training have left Ease Communication immediately upon receiving their certification. This is another way that the company is not getting their money back from the training they provide: interpreters-in-training get all the training and mentoring from certified interpreters and earn money during their training period and then leave once they are certified. Understandably, Ease Communication needs some way to recoup the money they spend on interpreters-in-training; the company allows trainees to take calls on their own sooner so they can bill the FCC for the trainees' time.

Since they are not certified sign language interpreters, Ease Communication pays interpreters-in-training anywhere from $10 to $18 less per hour than a certified interpreter. It should be noted that even at $20 per hour, trainees are earning considerable money without holding any credentials in interpreting. However, they are still earning less than they would if they were to interpret outside of VRS without any credentials. In addition, the use of noncertified interpreters is not unique to Ease Communication or to VRS. Many agencies have an increasing pool of noncertified interpreters working for them.[10]

10. In response to the growing use of noncertified interpreters some states have passed legislation requiring interpreters to hold national certification to work in their state.

The licensure issue raises questions of jurisdiction for VRS. For example, when an interpreter is working in Arizona but interpreting for callers in the state of New York, and the state of Arizona requires a license to interpret but New York does not, which state law should apply? When the law was proposed and later passed in Arizona, the rationale was to provide protection for members of the Arizona Deaf community. As a state legislation, it covers only the practice of interpreting in the state of Arizona. I was told by one manager that Ease Communication requires all interpreters in states with licensure requirements to hold a license to "cover their bases." Although this may be the stated policy for Ease Communication, I have heard of interpreters working without such license in VRS centers.

Scheduler

The scheduler is a part of the operations department and is therefore supervised by the operations director, who is in the national office. In both of the centers, the scheduler is someone who is not an interpreter.[11] Initially, the scheduler did just what the title suggested. Schedulers were responsible for filling time slots with the required number of interpreters. They were told by the national office the number of interpreters needed, and they would contact interpreters and see who was available and willing to take which shifts. This process has become more automated now, causing the scheduler's duties to change.

Schedulers are no longer responsible for contacting interpreters to fill shifts. Interpreters are now able to log into a system through the Internet and see which shifts need to be covered and place a bid. The stated practice is that the scheduler then approves the bid based on the interpreter's seniority.

Although schedulers have a great deal of control over the amount of work an interpreter gets, they do not have any supervisory responsibility and have very little, if any, interaction with the interpreters. Furthermore, the scheduler was often the focus of hostility from interpreters. In fact, many of the interpreters I spoke with talked about the fact that the scheduler who worked in their center seemed to them to be extremely incompetent. The interpreters were often angry with the scheduler because they did not get the schedule they wanted.

---

11. This is common even outside of video relay service. Many schedulers who work for referral agencies are not sign language interpreters.

The control a scheduler is able to exert over interpreters depends on the status of the interpreter. That is, full-time employees have a set schedule; they work the same days and same time every week. Unless an interpreter takes a vacation, her schedule does not change. Part-time interpreters and freelancers are much less consistent. As a part-time employee, I would be able to view the shifts that needed to be covered by logging into the computer system. This can be done while at a center or from my home. These shifts are in thirty-minute increments. Once I have submitted the schedule I want, the scheduler then is able to approve or deny my request. The scheduler's decision is based on the needs of the center and whether someone else has also requested the same schedule. Seniority also affects the schedule an interpreter gets.

Part-time and freelance interpreters are not guaranteed a minimum number of hours each week. Part-time employees who have the higher seniority are able to request the more ideal schedules. New or freelance employees are given the hours that are left. This provides an incentive for people to become and remain employees rather than independent contractors. It also encourages part-time employees to become full-time so that they can get a set schedule. This benefits Ease Communication because then they can be assured that the employee will cover 32 hours a week. Even though they would provide benefits to full-time employees, the amount of money they would be able to earn based on billable minutes generated by a full-time interpreter would be substantially more.

Even though it is stated that seniority is used to determine schedules, one interpreter, Kathryn, told me that she does not believe schedulers take seniority into consideration.

> I have been working here for nearly five years. I was one of the first interpreters hired on here. [. . .] Don't you think that would make my seniority high? Well I do. But I know for a fact that there are other interpreters who have been here less time than me and still get the schedules they want and I don't always get the schedules I want.

When asked whether Kathryn had confronted management about the inconsistency she witnessed, she stated:

> Yeah, I asked. I have asked several times. The first time I was told that it was based on seniority. Then after a couple of weeks of not getting the schedule I wanted and seeing others with less seniority getting the

schedules they wanted, I went back and talked to the manager. He then said, that it was not only based on seniority but they also considered a person's [billable minutes].

Kathryn's experience could have been due to the scheduling needs of the center. Whether an interpreter is meeting the numbers of a center does not change when interpreters are needed. Most businesses, including VRS, have peak hours and off hours. Kathryn's ideal schedule may have been during the off hours when they did not need additional people.

Management is also responsible for seeing the big picture. Because we do not have management's account of this situation, it is not clear if there are other reasons for not giving Kathryn the schedule she wants. It is not unreasonable to assume that management may have information that Kathryn does not, such as when others are available to work. Regardless of the reason, it has been communicated to Kathryn that based on her numbers she should have the schedule she wants. Her frustration comes from the seemingly arbitrary awarding of schedules. Regardless of management's motivation, inconsistencies in adherence to policies can be just as frustrating as strict adherence.

Kathryn is the only person who complained about the seniority issue. In my own experience, I was always given the schedule I wanted at one center but at another center I was often not given my ideal schedule. Given that I was working for Ease Communication two years before the second center was opened, I figured I would have the highest seniority. When I asked management about this, I was told that seniority only counts at the first center worked at. That is, because I started at another center, I would have high seniority there but since others had started working at the second center before me, they had higher seniority. I never pressed the issue.

Manager

The manager is responsible for the day-to-day operations of the center. Managers are responsible for hiring interpreters and for seeing that there are enough interpreters to cover the call volume. Even though they are responsible for making sure there are enough interpreters to answer the calls, managers do not supervise schedulers, a point that has irritated at least two managers with whom I spoke who complained about this. This is because managers' annual evaluations are dependent on whether they are able to staff the center with enough interpreters to cover the call volume for the day, which in turn depends on the schedulers' abilities to do their jobs. Since the managers' evaluations depend on the work of others, they feel they should also supervise the schedulers.

In both centers, the manager is also an interpreter.[12] In terms of the company, this comes in handy because the manager is also able to interpret calls, which will increase billable minutes. While I was working in one of the centers, I received a call that required two interpreters. It was a conference call that was going to continue for approximately two hours. All of the other interpreters in the center were on calls, and my manager was able to assist with the call.

While it is useful to have a manager who can help out when you are interpreting, it is also nice to have a manager who understands what it is you do. In discussing some of the dilemmas faced during a call, a manager who is also an interpreter is able to relate.

The field of sign language interpreting is very small and most interpreters in a particular area will know each other. The managers are chosen from the community in which the center is located, and this helps with recruitment of other interpreters. Often interpreters have worked with each other in a variety of settings. They have seen each other interact with members of the Deaf community and have had deaf people tell them about what they like and do not like about certain interpreters. A local interpreter who is hired as a manager knows the strengths and weaknesses of their colleagues. They are better equipped to assess whether a particular interpreter is going to meet the needs of the center and handle the type of calls they are likely to receive. Furthermore, when the manager is a respected and a well-liked colleague, as was the case in one center, she is able to staff the center with friends who are willing to work hard to make the manager look good.

The manager is also responsible for ensuring that new interpreters are trained. In some cases, new interpreters are assigned to an experienced interpreter who will train them. However, more often it is the manager who sits with the interpreter and walks them through the protocols for various calls. Once the interpreter is done with training, he will sit with an experienced interpreter and begin to take calls.

12. Only in one video relay service center where I worked was my direct supervisor not an interpreter.

Director

In addition to the manager and the scheduler, a three-tier center also has a director. Whereas managers are responsible for the day-to-day operations, directors may have managers at multiple centers who report to them. Even though the director is also an interpreter, he rarely does the training for the center; that is left to the manager.

Video Relay Provisional Coordinator and Other Support Personnel

Some centers also have trainers. These trainers, called interpreter-in-training coordinators, are responsible for training. The interpreter-in-training coordinator will also coordinate trainings for the rest of the interpreters. These people report to the national training department of Ease Communication, which is part of the national office.

Whether a center has an interpreter-in-training coordinator depends on whether it can support an interpreter-in-training program. If there is enough need (i.e., an abundance of noncertified interpreters available), then a center can request to be considered for the interpreter-in-training program. This is not dependent on whether the center is organized in two or three tiers.

Some centers also house technical support staff. The technical support staff responds to both internal and external customers. They do not report to any person within the center. Like the interpreter-in-training coordinator, whether a center houses technical support staff does not depend on the tier category of the center, but on other factors, such as size of the facility.

CLAIMING SPACE

Interpreters in VRS centers carry out their work in cubicles. The cubicles are not assigned to individual interpreters, officially. However, interpreters who have the same schedule each week or who are employed by Ease Communication as staff employees rather than independent contractors will typically sit in the same cubicle and decorate it with their personal artifacts. To ward off would-be squatters, interpreters place their name and scheduled hours outside the cubicle. There is a sense of ownership over the space and some interpreters become territorial. At times, this practice leads to animosity and outright hostility among interpreters.

Kathryn, an interpreter with over fifteen years of experience, has been working at Ease Communication for nearly five years. Here Kathryn describes a situation that occurred when one interpreter asked another interpreter to leave "her" cubicle:

> You see, the part-timers can't get a regular station, but the full-timers can. Sheila, I think she was a part-timer . . . yeah she was a part-timer. Well, Eleanor [who is a full-timer] came in one day and she always sat in [station] 11. Well that day, Sheila was sitting in the station. Eleanor told [Sheila] to leave. [Eleanor] said, "I am here now and this is my station."

Even though every interpreter can, and many do, bring family photos or other personal items to place in the cubicle they are working in, part-time and freelance interpreters do not have an assigned cubicle that they will use every time they work. The unspoken policy, which varies among centers, is that full-timers get to use the same station when they are working.

As Kathryn continues, she says that even though Sheila was on a call, rather than finding another station to sit in, Eleanor stood next to the cubicle, presumably to hurry Sheila along. Sheila told Eleanor to leave—which she did, but not until she was able to collect her personal items, such as pictures that were in the station.

A sense of ownership is one reason that interpreters may have an affinity for a particular station. Another reason is that the station may be set up in such a way that makes it conducive for the interpreter to perform her or his work. For example, one part-time interpreter, Marianne, explained that she only likes to use the stations that have the computer on the right of the television screen. She also does not like to use the select stations that have the ergonomically correct keyboards because she has "trouble typing on those types of keyboards." I, on the other hand, did not mind the ergonomic keyboards, but I typically chose a cubicle that was further away from the place where interpreters may congregate to discuss schedules, wait for a station to become available, or read the various notices posted on the wall.

Although allowing interpreters to claim dominion over a particular station for either comfort or consistency provides interpreters with a sense of belonging, it seems counter to other aspects of VRS work that aim to reduce individuality and promote interchangeability. The goal is to create an environment in which any interpreter can use any cubicle and produce billable minutes. Assigning cubicles to particular interpreters and allowing them to place personal belongings in the cubicles reduces the interchangeability. On the other hand, as Kupritz (1999) suggests, personalizing one's space may produce a more productive worker.

Shared Spaces

In addition to the individual cubicles that are designed for interpreting phone calls, there are other shared spaces throughout the centers. These spaces have a particular function. One particular space is the break room. The break rooms provide needed respites from calls and interpreting. Interpreters who are on break at the same time can gather in the break rooms and recount information about particular calls. Even though interpreters are not supposed to provide details of calls, most interpreters would provide enough information that others who had experience with a particular caller would know exactly who was being discussed. This was often followed by others chiming in to tell about their last experience with that particular caller. Many times these callers were given descriptive nicknames. For example, one caller who liked to call and show the tip of his penis to the female interpreters was called "Dick Head," a name that is both descriptive and insulting.

Female interpreters would sit in the break room and tell stories about their recent call with Dick Head. Often interpreters would giggle and provide each other with support as to how to handle Dick Head's calls. On one occasion a new interpreter was being warned about Dick Head:

> Diane: You are working late tonight, right?
> Kimberly: Well, you will probably get a call from Dick Head tonight.
> Diane: Really? What should I do?
> Kimberly: It is up to you but I usually just hang up on him and send an email to whoever is in charge. They can deal with it. He really is harmless but he just likes to show you his dick.
> Cathy (interrupts): Yeah, I just hang up on him.
> Diane: I don't want to see that. (giggles). I will just hang up.

Even though there is no discussion of the identity of Dick Head, both Kimberly and Cathy know who he is. This is because it is not uncommon to get calls from the same caller while working a particular shift. This is more likely to occur during the graveyard shift because there are fewer centers open and fewer interpreters working.

Other times interpreters talk in generalities and the intent is much more cathartic. For example, Tina tears up as she walks into the break room and, talking to nobody in particular, relives the call she recently received:

Wow! That was hard. I just had a call between a boy at college and his mother. He was yelling at his mother. He was telling her that she really hurt him because she never learned sign language. He said that he was glad that he went to a residential school so that he didn't have to be around people who didn't talk to him. He then said that the Deaf community was his real family.

Even though Tina does not address anyone in particular, we all listen intently to her story. Then Beth Ann asks, "What did his mother say?" As Tina tries to regain her composure, she says, "She said she knew. She said that there was nothing she could do—that she didn't know any better." As if she just could feel the boy's pain, she says, "and then the mother just said, 'Listen, Keith. You have been calling me for a month now complaining about this. Why haven't you gotten over it yet?'" At this point, every person in the room started to provide their opinion on the subject. These opinions were in support of both Tina for having to endure the emotional call and Keith for having to endure his mother's ignorance. Nobody in the room spoke in support of the mother.

Another shared space is called the Floater Station, where interpreters wait for a station to open up. Here they can log onto the computer, surf the Internet, and submit their timecards and invoices. The Floater Station is not a separate space like the break rooms, so discussions are rather minimal. However, people do use the time here to catch up with colleagues they have not seen for some time.

TECHNOLOGICAL INTERFACE

Aside from the physical environment, computer technology has a significant role in organizing the work of interpreters in this setting. Technology is abundant in most offices in a postindustrial society. In VRS centers, computer technology is used to distribute calls and to predict call volume, among other tasks. The information gathered to perform these two tasks is also used to create schedules.

An indispensable component of a call center is the automatic call distribution (ACD) program (Taylor and Bain 1999). ACD programs not only direct calls to available interpreters but they can also generate reports that calculate the number of calls received per minute, predict call volume, and calculate the number of interpreters needed for a given time period. The number of interpreters needed for a given time is made available to interpreters who can then bid for shifts.

While ACD programs have streamlined the scheduling process for Ease Communication and lessened wait times for callers, these programs also strip interpreters of their discretion. Instead of depending on interpreters to determine their ability to provide an accurate interpretation, a computer program determines when and how many interpreters are needed at any given time. The current computer program does not evaluate whether the interpreters they are scheduling are the most qualified to provide interpreting; this means that a concern for covering the calls dictates who works, rather than interpreters' professional judgment.

Call Distribution

Now, all calls to VRS centers, originating from anywhere in the world, go into a national queue. However, because the FCC reimburses VRS providers for calls, for funding purposes at least one of the parties must be in the United States.[13] The call is then routed to the next available station and interpreter.

When I first began working at Ease Communication, calls were routed locally so three or four centers shared the same queue and the technology was such that I was able to see those callers waiting in the queue. That is, I could see the number they were calling to and from and I could see the name the phone assigned to the videophone used to place the call. This capability allowed me to see if the next caller was someone I could, or wanted to, work with, as well as see how long they had been waiting in the queue. In some cases, if the deaf person who was next in line to receive an interpreter was someone I knew and for whom I felt I would not be the best interpreter, based on my skill or his language needs, I chose to take the next person in line. If several interpreters did this, a caller could be waiting in the queue for several minutes. The FCC determined that this was tantamount to preferential treatment and ordered that the practice

---

13. Occasionally, both the caller and the person being called are located in other countries, such as Canada, where various video relay service providers have distributed their equipment widely. When this occurs, Ease Communication policy states that the call must be terminated, politely, but immediately.

be discontinued. Now, calls are distributed based on when the interpreter logged in. The goal is that the interpreter who has been available the longest gets the next call. This practice helps with burnout. Some providers still have technology that allows the interpreters to see the next person in the queue and are able to see how long the person has been waiting, but it limits how often interpreters can "jump the queue" and skip the person who is next in line to receive an interpreter.

The call volume is higher on certain days. Typically Mondays and Tuesdays are the busiest. In addition, certain holidays, such as Mother's Day, are extremely busy. The call distribution program helps on these days, but interpreters are still answering calls back to back. Because the hold time for callers is longer on these days, callers are more likely to be disgruntled when they finally get an interpreter. Some interpreters have chosen to avoid working on these days. On these days when the call volume is expected to be high, Ease Communication offers incentive pay to entice interpreters to work.

Scheduling

The scheduling process for Ease Communication has changed over the years. In the beginning, schedulers were responsible for scheduling individual interpreters by hand. As the technology has advanced, schedulers' jobs have been limited to approving and denying schedule bids.

People's schedules determine what they can do in a given day, week, month, and year. Interpreters cited the schedule as one of the benefits of working in VRS. More than once I was told that VRS is an ideal source of interpreting income because some interpreters can get the same schedule every week. Every VRS center I worked for schedules interpreters a month in advance, which allows interpreters to know their schedules in advance, at least for the month.

Even if interpreters are not guaranteed a particular schedule, there is certain amount of consistency with video relay interpreting. The pool of consumers, deaf and non-deaf, is large and not limited by geographical area as it is in-person interpreting. Also in contrast to in-person interpreting, video relay interpreters know exactly how much money is coming in, and they are able to schedule other jobs and errands accordingly. Furthermore, unless the technology goes down there are no cancellations in VRS. Also, since some VRS centers are open 24 hours a day and 365 days a year, interpreters can depend on video relay for a paycheck when other types of work are scarce, such as during the summer and holiday season.

As a sign language interpreter, I am used to being at the beck and call of other people's schedules. Although I could limit my working hours to a 9:00 A.M. to 5:00 P.M., Monday through Friday, schedule, that would reduce the income I could earn. There is a lot of business that deaf people take care of during those hours; however, there are situations when deaf people use the services of an interpreter that do not occur between 9:00 A.M. and 5:00 P.M., Monday through Friday, such as emergencies or night classes. Therefore, most interpreters who are freelance practitioners have to be willing to work around the clock. This may mean that they interpret a medical emergency at 2:00 A.M. and an 8:00 A.M. board meeting later the same day.

Interpreting in video relay service is clearly call-center work. According to Hinrichs, Roche, and Sirianni (1991), "For increasing numbers of employees the length of the working day and working week is becoming a variable or flexible feature of employment, influenced primarily by the pattern of demand confronting the firms in which they work" (4). In call centers, employees' schedules are dependent on call volume.

When Ease Communication started providing VRS, scheduling interpreters was center-specific. That is, the national office knew how many interpreters were needed during any given period and would attempt to distribute those among all of the centers. No one center knew how many interpreters were needed nationwide for a given time period. For example, if there were ten interpreters needed from 9:00 A.M. to 9:30 A.M., one center might be responsible for finding two interpreters while another would be responsible for locating four, and still another center would be charged with scheduling four more. However, if one of those centers was unable to find the right number of interpreters, then other centers would be bombarded with calls to compensate for the number of interpreters who were not scheduled for that time slot.

Another problem that could occur was that one center might be able to schedule five interpreters but had only been allotted three slots; therefore, two interpreters would be turned away. Since interpreters talk with one another, as do all employees, about their shifts (not the call contents but the call volume), it is not uncommon to hear some interpreters complaining about the number of calls they had during a given shift while another complains that she or he asked to work and was turned down. A manager, Jake, explained the process to me:

> We don't decide the number of interpreters we schedule. That informa-
> tion comes from headquarters. So they tell us that we need to schedule

four interpreters, for example, and we do it. The problem is that if they would say, for example, that we need 120 interpreters from this time to this time then each center could schedule as many interpreters as they could until the whole 120 slots are filled. But how it works now is that they tell us to schedule four, they tell St. Louis to schedule fifteen, and then they tell [the center in] Houston to schedule six. Well then once we have scheduled our four, if other interpreters want to work we have to turn them away because we already have the four interpreters we need.

Now that Jake has explained the process, he continues by explaining the problems inherent in the current process.

Now the problem happens because maybe we got the four people, but St. Louis only got twelve of the people they needed. So then the interpreters here get slammed with calls. We are all connected, but headquarters doesn't want to give up control over that. It would just be easier if they had a set number like the 120 and just let each site schedule as many interpreters as possible until the whole 120 was covered. That way if we have a lot of interpreters available then we could cover more than the four slots they allotted us. So we should all have the same size site; for example, we should all have twenty-five stations.

Jake's recommendation would mean that some interpreters would not be able to get any work since scheduling would be done on a first come, first served basis. Furthermore, because the centers are not the same size those areas with larger centers and larger pools of interpreters would fill more quickly than the smaller ones.

As a manager, Jake must deal with the impact of not having enough interpreters. If there is not enough downtime or time when an interpreter can catch his breath between calls, burnout is more likely. As such, it behooves management, to an extent, to increase the time that interpreters are not processing calls. To do this, there must be more interpreters available to take calls so that the time between calls per interpreter is extended. In addition to the frustration experienced by managers and burnout by interpreters, there may be an increased holding time for callers that could violate the "speed of answer" required by the FCC.

The "speed of answer" is a measurement of the total number of seconds a call can remain in queue. The goal of the relay, text and video, is to make the telephone experience of deaf people more functionally equivalent to that of non-deaf people. Kelby Brick, director of law and advocacy for the National Association of the Deaf (NAD), along with the other members of the National Video Relay Service Coalition,[14] stated in a comment to the FCC:

> Deaf and hard of hearing customers are tired of long waits before they can call anybody. Speed of answer rules will provide customers with access to telephone services and be a step closer to the Americans with Disabilities Act (ADA)'s requirement for functional equivalency. (www.nad.org)

As a result of this comment, and others, the FCC required that by January 1, 2007, VRS providers would answer 80 percent of all calls, calculated monthly, within 120 seconds, in order to receive remuneration from the National Exchange Carrier Association. This standard assumes a great deal about the interpreting that occurs within VRS centers. First, it assumes that interpreters do not call in sick for work. When this happens, there is going to be one less interpreter available to respond to calls. Furthermore, it puts additional strain on those interpreters who are working. This means that they may experience a greater amount of burnout or fatigue. When this happens, interpreters may be apt to take more breaks during the day. This would undoubtedly increase callers' wait time.

This regulation also assumes that there is an "average" call, with relatively little divergence from the typical call length. However, there is no way to know how long a call will take. The VRS Task Analysis Report, completed by the Distance Opportunities for Interpreter Training (DO IT) Center at the University of Northern Colorado in 2005, found that "there is no limit to the types of calls that require interpretation" (10). Calls may range from brief calls in which a caller informs a friend or family member that they are on their way to more lengthy calls that include several people discussing in detail a business agenda for nearly two hours. Although the first type of call would not interfere with adhering

14. The National Video Relay Service Coalition is an ad hoc group that includes the following organizations: Telecommunications for the Deaf, Deaf and Hard of Hearing Consumer Advocacy Network, National Association of the Deaf, the Association for Late Deafened Adults, the American Association of People with Disabilities, Deaf and Hard of Hearing in Government, the California Coalition of Agencies Serving the Deaf and Hard of Hearing, the Student Body Government of Gallaudet University, and the Registry of Interpreters for the Deaf.

to the speed of answer regulations, the second would mean that at least one interpreter, or two if the call was difficult, would not be able to assist with incoming calls for nearly two hours.

Furthermore, standard practice in the field of sign language interpreting is that two interpreters work as a team for any job that requires more than one and a half hours of constant interpreting. This means that when an interpreter receives a call that is likely to go beyond the hour-and-a-half threshold,[15] such as a business conference call, she automatically calls on another interpreter to assist with the call. Another interpreter can also be called on for assistance if the interpreter who receives a call feels he cannot effectively interpret the call on his own, for example, if a deaf caller is difficult to understand because of cerebral palsy, muscular dystrophy, or any other distracting motor impairment, or if a deaf caller uses a particular dialect of sign language that is particularly difficult to understand. A non-deaf caller may have a thick accent that the interpreter cannot understand, or there may be a lot of background noise. All of these situations can lengthen the speed of answer of future calls while the interpreters work to provide a quality interpretation.

To meet the minimum standards set by the FCC, each center must account for interpreters calling in sick, for spikes in calls, and for calls that require more time to complete. Individual schedulers have taken up different ways to meet the needs of the centers and also adhere to Ease Communication's own policies. For example, in anticipation of situations like those described above, schedulers schedule additional interpreters. Sue, a scheduler at one of the centers, explained to me how the process of scheduling worked:

> We can schedule three [interpreters] over our target. So you can see (as she points to the schedule in front of her) here, I only needed five interpreters but I scheduled seven. Later, I needed three but I only had two. Hopefully another center was able to schedule over their target.

Sue's practice of scheduling more interpreters for a given time period than she needed is one way the different centers exert control over their work. Even though she did not contact the other centers to tell them she

---

15. All of the VRS centers that I have worked in and heard about have technology built into the computers that indicate to the interpreters that it is time to take a break after twenty minutes.

was unable to fill all her slots, she was "hopeful" that they overschedule when they can, like she does. Scheduling over the number of allotted interpreters at one time and not being able to find enough interpreters at another time balances out in the end.

The scheduling system focuses on numbers and was developed and implemented by people at headquarters who have likely never worked in a VRS center as interpreters; therefore, it is unlikely they understand the full ramifications of the practice. The process of scheduling at Ease Communication continues to evolve. The technology that predicts call volumes has become more sophisticated and thus has reduced the flexibility of video relay schedulers. Rather than allot individual centers a portion of the needed interpreters, people at headquarters now put out a call for a total number of interpreters needed during a given time, just as Jake suggested. As interpreters are scheduled or schedule themselves via the online bidding system for these shifts, the number of available slots is decreased by one automatically. This ensures a more accurate accounting of the number of interpreters needed and hired for a given time period.

In order for the various forms of technology to work successfully, there must be an accurate tracking of interpreters and the time interpreters are available to accept calls. To track this, management uses various texts to make interpreters and the system accountable. The Log, according to Sue, is a mechanism used by the scheduler to "adjust" interpreters' time sheets. Much like the practice of balancing one's checkbook, the scheduler cross-references the report produced as interpreters log in and out, also known as the Productivity Report, and the Log. Although this practice is referred to as "adjusting," it is actually a way for Ease Communication to accurately reflect what interpreters are doing and accurately bill the FCC. I will discuss these tracking and surveillance texts in more detail in chapter 5.

Once interpreters are inside the center and have begun to work at a station, they continue to interface with various machines and programs that are used to produce a textual account of their presence in the center, and connect them to other interpreters and to the callers.

Instant Messaging

The call distribution program is not the only technology interpreters interface with while performing the task of processing calls. Because interpreters, while sitting in their cubicles, may be unable to see if someone needs assistance, is on break, has left for the day, or is available to help out on a call, Ease Communication uses Instant Messaging (IM) technology so that interpreters can "see" who else is in the center and keep track of them.

After logging into the computer, but before accepting calls, interpreters are supposed to log into the IM program. Using the IM program, they can see how many interpreters are on break and whether the ratio of interpreters working to interpreters on break is such that they can take a break. One document that is taped to the wall in the cubicle is a document that explains how to use the Instant Messaging program correctly. It provides interpreters with information about what "Online," "Busy," "Be Right Back," and other statuses mean. It also outlines how many people can be on break at one time. This practice ensures there are enough interpreters available to take calls.

As I discussed earlier, the IM program also allows interpreters to "see" who is available to assist with a call or who is the point of contact for the center if there is no supervisor on site. This is useful when a caller wants to talk to a supervisor to file a complaint or provide praise. In actuality, the person acting as a supervisor is another interpreter who has agreed to be the point of contact for the center.

Each interpreter in the center is assigned Point of Contact (POC) duty on a rotating basis. Any person, except an interpreter-in-training, can be a POC. The POC usually is only the POC for three or four hours of her or his shift. There is no pay increase for doing this and no additional authority. The ability to call on someone else who is the acting supervisor allows interpreters to give the perception that they are elevating a caller to the next level. In addition, interpreters are able to contact one another when they are unable to understand either the deaf caller or non-deaf caller and ask for assistance. This is all done by sending IMs back and forth. While interpreters can refuse to be the POC for a number of reasons, it does provide interpreters with additional responsibilities and perceived authority. For this reason, few interpreters refuse POC duty.

Not only can interpreters use this system to "observe" their colleagues, but they can send IMs to each other, as a group or individually. During slow times, I carried on conversations with interpreters in the center that ranged from my plans for the weekend to participating in my dissertation research. In some cases, interpreters "meet" each other for the first time in cyberspace. In this way, this technology allows interpreters to feel connected to one another despite the isolating layout of the center.

After logging into the computer and the IM program, making sure they are on camera, and fitting their headsets on, interpreters are ready to begin accepting calls. Again, because the schedule is carefully calculated to ensure there are just enough interpreters to cover the predicted call volume, the wait for a call is typically minimal.

Call Setup

"Call setup" refers to the period when the interpreter is connected to only one of the callers and has not dialed the intended party. This is the time when the caller (deaf or non-deaf) communicates with the interpreter before the other individual is called. This period includes the deaf caller telling the interpreter what number to call and who to ask for, the actual dialing of the number, and the phone ringing or giving a busy signal.

Those first few seconds of interaction between the deaf caller and the interpreter are crucial to a successful call. When a caller is already annoyed because she has had to wait for an interpreter, the interpreter's ability to defuse the situation immediately helps ensure the call will go smoothly. Otherwise, the tension could run over into the call.

Billable Time

VRS providers cannot bill the FCC until both callers are connected. Therefore, to ensure that VRS providers can bill for the interpreter's time, once a call appears on an interpreter's computer screen and is accepted (i.e., not returned to queue) the computer initiates a clock. This clock tallies that amount of time the interpreters spend "setting up the call." After thirty seconds the clock begins to flash on the computer screen to remind the interpreter that he has not placed an outgoing call yet and is not billable. Here is an example from my field notes of such a situation:

> The deaf woman comes up on my screen. She seems nice. She is older. I would say she is in her early seventies. (I am not good at determining age.) The woman says, "Hello." I respond, "Hello. Thank you for using Ease Communication, Inc. I am interpreter number 9999." The woman tells me that I sign very well. She then tells me that she is going to call her doctor. She continues, "I was supposed to call my doctor yesterday but I got busy. Then when I got home it was too late. I hope they are not upset that I didn't call yesterday." Halfway through the

caller's explanation, the computer begins to flash. I can see it in my peripheral vision and know that it is warning me that I am not billable. I choose to ignore the flashing light and continue with the brief dialogue with the caller.

Deaf people are often isolated in a world of nonsigning people. Therefore, it is not uncommon for deaf people to use VRS as a way to interact with someone who understands their language. While in the break room, I heard many interpreters talk about the "sweet old lady who didn't really have to make a call but wanted to talk with someone." Nobody I spoke with ever told me that they told the caller they could not talk.

Types of Calls

During a shift interpreters interpret for a variety of calls: a deaf person calling a family member, an office manager of a doctor's office calling a deaf patient to confirm her appointment for the following day, a conference call between executives. There is no guarantee, but calls of a business nature are more likely to occur, for obvious reasons, between the hours of 8:00 A.M. and 5:00 P.M., and calls of a more personal nature (e.g., calling to ask someone out on a date) are more likely to occur after 5:00 P.M. Still, because interpreters are working with people all over the world and in varied time zones, "expecting the unexpected" is a terrific motto to adopt. In fact, the DO IT Center (2005) found that adaptability was one of the competencies necessary in VRS interpreting:

> Along with experience, interpreters must be quick minded. [. . .] For example, calls may be made that are very familiar to interpreters, such as calling a doctor's office to set up an appointment for an annual physical examination, or calling a secretary at a school to notify the teacher that their son, Pete, is sick and will not be attending school. Other kinds of calls are more difficult to interpret, for example, when colleagues are talking to each other using acronyms that are unfamiliar to interpreters. Or when several callers are on the line for a conference call, it may be difficult to identify who is talking, in addition to what they are talking about if it is highly technical or heavily laden with inside humor. (10)

Indeed, most interpreters who work in VRS have placed a call to a doctor's office or a child's school. And, most interpreters have interpreted a phone call between a deaf person and her boss. Interpreters have more than likely had both personal and professional experience in each of these settings; therefore, it is not difficult to conceptualize the contents of a meeting and use closure skills (defined below) to fill in when certain information is not presented. However, it is at times when interpreters do not have any experience or knowledge that they can use to fill in a context for the call that they typically struggle with providing a successful interpretation.

Closure skills, or what Oller refers to as "active hypothesis testing" (cited in Patrie 2000, 197) are perhaps an interpreter's best friend in all kinds of interpreting situations. Every interpreter, indeed every person, uses closure skills, meaning the drawing on previous knowledge and common sense to fill in gaps in understanding. In interpreting, the gaps occur when the interpreter does not have all of the information that those for whom they are interpreting have. For example, a deaf person places a call to her doctor. The doctor answers the phone and says, "Hello Mrs. Smith." The deaf caller states, "Hello doctor. It's back." The doctor then responds, "Oh. OK. Well, do you still have the ointment? Have you put it on it?" In ASL, the pronoun "it" does not exist. While the doctor and the patient both know what "it" is, the interpreter must wait until some clue is given to provide an accurate interpretation. Furthermore, because ASL is visual, the interpreter must know where "it" is on the body so that he can properly interpret "putting it on."

In some cases, the interpreter will ask what "it" is. In other situations, the interpreter may wait until she can figure out what "it" is. If this is not stated explicitly, the interpreter must rely on her closure skills to interpret. Sometimes this is easy. The interpreter may remember that the call was placed to a podiatrist and therefore "it" is something on or around the feet. However, if the call is being placed to a dermatologist and the deaf person has severe acne on her face, the signed language interpreter could assume that "it" is some form of acne but where exactly on the body may not be clear. In this situation, the interpreter could guess or just wait until more information is provided. Either way, the interpreter uses closure skills to determine meaning not provided in the original statements.

Identity in VRS

The FCC aims to have a transparent interpreter. Interpreters are supposed to provide access without influencing the outcome of the situation. This ignores the fact that adding a person, even one who attempts to stay neutral, changes the dynamics of the interaction. At times, I have felt that compliance with the FCC's drive to have interpreters remain "non-people" has been more disruptive than helpful.

People are uncomfortable when they are unable to get a name from someone they are talking to. In America, at least, it is a cultural norm to introduce yourself when you first meet someone. This is also a norm within Deaf culture. On more than one occasion, I have been asked by both the deaf caller and the non-deaf person for my name. For the most part, deaf people are aware that we are unable to give them any part of our names. However, there is other information that they ask for that we are asked not to provide. Karen, an interpreter, explains why she believes we should not give our names or other identifying information:

> We could get stalked. We don't want the deaf person to show up at the center and want to talk with the interpreter. You know how sometimes deaf people get attached to the interpreter and want to use them all the time for everything. If they knew we were in their city they may try to find us. Also, [our center is] open all night and that means that it could be dangerous for some people.

Karen states that there have been stalking situations, but she does not know any of the details. However, Margaret, who is a director of one of the centers, explains, "It is easier for you to not get involved if they don't have your name. If all they know is your number you don't have to engage them." Jake, however, says that this practice is a "hold over from the text relay." And it "doesn't have anything to do with stalking."

Even though interpreters have been told to refrain from providing specific information about ourselves to our callers, there are times when I feel it is a good idea to provide the information. In some cases, interpreters are interpreting in very private and personal situations. I would not want to divulge intimate details about myself (e.g., social security number, health status, financial problems) without knowing to whom I was talking. At times, however, providing personal information can tend to produce an "us versus them" alliance with the deaf caller. During my shift at Ease Communication in April of 2006 the following occurred:

> The deaf caller is asking me what time it is where I am. Without thinking I tell her. She then asks where I am. I tell her I am in New York. She tells me not to worry that she will not tell anyone that I have told her where I am. She then winks at me.

This exchange occurred while the non-deaf person had placed us on hold. The breach of protocol on my part did not disrupt the rest of the call, in my opinion. Although Ease Communication was able to bill for the time in the example above, the practice of conversing with the deaf or non-deaf caller before or during the call about things personal in nature is prohibited. Furthermore, any discussion after one of the callers has disconnected is also prohibited.

Deaf people use VRS on a much more frequent basis than non-deaf persons. As such, non-deaf persons are often uncomfortable when they ask us our names and we give them a number. On the same day that I told the deaf caller that I was in New York, a non-deaf person called and asked me my name:

A non-deaf person asks my name. I tell him that I am interpreter number 9999. He asks me again. I explain that I am not allowed to give him my name but that he can use my number, 9999, to identify me if there is a need to.

Often this explanation suffices and the call proceeds. However, occasionally the deaf caller is conducting business with a bank or a social security office and the non-deaf person wants more information because he does not trust that I am actually interpreting for a deaf patron. In such a case, the prescription for neutrality seems to produce obstacles to accomplishing the goals of all parties involved.

Sign language interpreters convey the communications of the people for whom they are interpreting in first person. That is, when a deaf person signs, "HELLO MY NAME MARCOS. ME WANT TALK DANIEL," the interpreter will say, "Hello, my name is Marcos. I want to talk to Daniel." In VRS, it is customary for interpreters to identify the process but not themselves. Therefore, even though we are talking in first person, the non-deaf person has been told that it is not actually the deaf person calling. When the non-deaf person answers the phone, we read the following script:[16]

Hello. This is interpreter number _____ with Ease Communication, Inc. I have a video relay call (from a customer, patient, etc.) for you. Have you received a video relay call before?

16. These scripts are not the exact scripts used by Ease Communication. Furthermore, each VRS provider has its own scripts, and each one that I have seen gives basically the same information.

If the non-deaf caller says, "Yes, I have had a video relay call before," the interpreter will say, "I will connect you with the caller," and the call continues. If, on the other hand, they have not, there is another script we read. That script says:

> I will briefly explain. I have a person on the line who uses sign language to communicate. We can see each other on TV screens. I will be interpreting the call between the two of you. You don't need to say "GA" or "go ahead." I will connect the caller.

The interpreter can, and does, in certain situations elaborate on the script. For example, we do not always include the phrase about "GA" or "go ahead," which relates to the turn-taking practices used in text relay service. It is only when the non-deaf caller is familiar with text relay but not video relay that interpreters typically include this reference. The interpreter can change the words used to convey the other parts of the scripts.

However, there is one place where we are told not to elaborate: with the line that states, "I have a person on the line who uses sign language to communicate." Because the issue of identity is touchy, we are told not to replace "sign language" with "American Sign Language" or say that the person on the line is "deaf." Both of these imply a cultural affinity. Therefore, we are told to state only that the caller uses sign language, something we can see, and not to make a judgment as to whether they consider themselves to be deaf or that their version of sign language is ASL.

Once the scripts are read, the call will proceed. It is the use of these scripts that can cause some problems with certain institutions, such as banks. Typically they are not willing to discuss financial information through a third party. I have, on several occasions, been asked to put the deaf person on the phone so he can give the bank personnel permission to talk with me about his finances because of confidentiality reasons. When I explain that I am providing a service and that the deaf person is not in the same room with me, bank personnel often refuse to cooperate. This is easily rectified by us calling back and not identifying the process. That is, I do not explain that there is a deaf person calling through an interpreter. I, and several of my colleagues, simply tell the deaf person that they should call back and not tell the person about VRS. Sometimes the deaf caller already knows that this is the way around the inflexible bank official. Either way, access and "functional equivalency" is achieved by breaking the rules.

Return to Queue

Although the scheduling and other technologies make VRS convenient for some interpreters, working for VRS means relinquishing the ability to assess interpreting assignments and choose the ones for which they are best suited. However, the technology used by Ease Communication does permit interpreters to return a call to the queue if, for example, they know the deaf person and feel they are unable to provide effective and unbiased interpretation for the caller. When a call drops into the queue and shows up on an interpreter's screen, the interpreter can see the name of the caller, the phone number the caller is calling from, and the number she wishes to call. At this point, there is no visual of the deaf person, and she has not seen the interpreter. With a simple click of the mouse, the interpreter can drop the call back in the queue for the next available interpreter. Even though this capability is there, the practice seems to be frowned upon by management (and the FCC). Here Kathryn talks about how she uses the return-to-queue option:

> One of the reasons that I wanted to work at Ease Communication is because I didn't want to interpret for people locally anymore. I had interpreted for a lot of them. I knew most of them because of my parents [who are deaf]. But now that my husband is deaf too, I just feel like everybody is afraid that anything I interpret I am going to tell my husband. I just don't want to deal with it. That is why I return to queue. When I see a deaf person who I know drop into my station, I return it to queue so that I don't have to interpret for them.

Kathryn was eventually called into the manager's office and warned that she was abusing the return-to-queue option. The manager was not persuaded by Kathryn's argument. Kathryn told me that she thinks using this option for two or three calls per shift would be acceptable, but she was not sure. When I asked other interpreters about the practice of returning to queue, the answers varied. Tyler, an interpreter who is currently in graduate school, told me he too worked at Ease Communication so he would not have to interpret for local people anymore. "I am trying to distance myself from the local Deaf community because I am hoping to become a therapist in this community. I want them to see me as a therapist, not an interpreter." However, when I asked Tyler whether he had been talked to about using the return-to-queue option, he stated,

I try not to use it too much. Most of the time, I get calls from people in other states so it doesn't really matter. There have been a few times, like last week, I was working the graveyard shift and every other call was from someone I knew. I had to return to queue. Nobody has mentioned it to me, yet. Maybe they haven't gotten the report. (giggles)

Tyler continues by saying, "But I have heard of others who have used the return-to-queue a lot. Also during meetings [management] has said that we should not abuse the return-to-queue function."

I followed up with Jake, who is a manager at one of the centers. He said, "The return-to-queue function is not to be used all the time. We know that there are going to be times when an interpreter doesn't want to interpret for a particular person for whatever reason or that they just need a break." When I asked him how many times is acceptable to return a call to queue he said, "If you are returning more than ten calls to queue per week that is too many. I think that ten would be ok." Jake told me that there was not a "hard-and-fast rule," though.

As Jake said, most people stated they used the return-to-queue option when they finished a call they found particularly difficult and needed a break before taking another call and had not logged off before the next call dropped into their station. This is the intended use for the return-to queue function.

ENDING A SHIFT

One of the regulations established by the FCC is that calls cannot be transferred to another interpreter within the first ten minutes after connecting (47 C.F.R. § 64.604[v]). This is to prevent the unnecessary transferring of a caller. This means that once a call is accepted by an interpreter, he must stay with the call until it is complete or ten minutes has passed. This only becomes a problem at the end of a shift. Interpreters do not want to take a call at 3:53 P.M. if they are scheduled to leave at 4:00 P.M. To avoid this, and stay in compliance with the FCC's regulations, interpreters log out ten minutes before their shift is scheduled to end. These ten minutes are used to clean up their stations and turn in their Logs (which I discuss further in chapter 5).

In addition to filing paperwork and cleaning their stations, interpreters are often assigned specific chores to be responsible for during these ten minutes. These chores include cleaning the microwave, wiping down the refrigerator, rinsing out the coffee maker, or straightening up the magazines. Each interpreter is assigned a specific duty and must initial next to her or his name on the Duty Roster once the task is complete. Some interpreters, like Theodore, a freelance interpreter, refuse to clean up after their colleagues; Theodore sees this practice as arising from the manager's needs rather than those of the center:

> The contract that I signed says that I will come here and interpret calls. I don't clean up. I will clean up after myself. I don't clean up the microwave. If I were to use the microwave, ever, I would clean up my mess. If I drank the coffee I would clean up after myself but since I don't, I am not going to clean out the coffee maker, the refrigerator, or the microwave. Those duties are a result of the call center manager who is a neat freak and really irritated by messes. Which is the situation for a lot of the "policies" (air quotes) that we have here. They really aren't policies as much as they are personal preferences by management.

Most of the people I asked about the assigned duties laughed and said they typically just signed their initials. There were a few people who saw this as a part of working for Ease Communication and did it without complaint.

CONCLUSION

Here, I have laid out the environment in which VRS interpreting occurs, provided an overview of personnel in the center and their responsibilities, and described some of the work interpreters perform during an ordinary shift. Although each provider may choose to set up its offices a little differently, the underlying theme is that the call centers are designed to produce billable minutes and to be a space where people perform work. This is done by providing enough information in the cubicles so interpreters do not have to leave the cubicles and can continue to process calls. Additionally, the centers are set up in such a way that deaf callers can rest assured that their confidentiality is being maintained, although, occasionally interpreters circumvent the confidentiality procedures established by the FCC. Despite the isolating design of the centers, interpreters find ways to connect to one another; they use Instant Messaging, the technology that is intended to track them, to promote a sense of community in the center.

There are a lot of different people who occupy space in VRS centers. Each person has a function that, when done correctly, produces a service that deaf and non-deaf people can access. However, this also means that interpreters have to learn each person's role and function so that they can get the support they need, when they need it. Furthermore, scheduling that is intended to cover the unexpected call volume so that the center is in compliance with the regulations set by the FCC sometimes leads to interpreters stepping on one another, which can lead to tension. The Floater Station represents the recognition that there are going to be more interpreters than needed for a given shift. As in any community, there are territorial conflicts, which are exacerbated when population density is high.

All interpreters multitask. They are receiving a message in one language and producing its equivalent in another language in real time. They now find themselves having to master one more thing, technology. For some interpreters this can be a rather simple task, and for others it can be daunting. In this new method of service delivery, interpreters are regulated in such a way to produce a non-person who acts as a go-between for the deaf and non-deaf person. They find themselves without control over for whom and when they interpret. The call distribution program used by Ease Communication (and other VRS providers) does not take into account that interpreters are not interchangeable. There are times when an interpreter should not accept a call even if she is the next one scheduled to receive it.

With the advent of VRS, my colleague's statement about "interpreting everything from birth to death" is now more accurate. However, what was once thought of as a relationship between two people who do not share a language, and thus use the services of a third person (see Baker-Shenk 1991; Humphrey and Alcorn 1994; Hilder 1995; Stewart et al. 1998), must now be understood as a web of relationships that spans multiple locations and involves multiple actors who are not immediately present. In the chapters that follow, I continue to explore the roles and experiences of these multiple actors, as well as the regulatory policies and texts that coordinate their activities. In the next chapter, I report on deaf people's experiences with VRS.

Chapter 3

"VRS Puts Us on Equal Footing

with Hearing People"

The video relay service is intended to be used by Americans who use a sign language to communicate. This is not *all* deaf people. Quantifying any marginalized population, including people who are deaf, is as much about identity politics as it is about power. That is, who has the power to define, and what does the definition imply? Those who were born with the ability to hear and later became deaf or hard of hearing may be reluctant to disclose their disability. Others, who are born deaf, may not consider themselves to be disabled and therefore may not respond to questions on surveys that ask about "hearing disability." For these reasons, an exact number of deaf people in the United States is difficult to come by. In 1992 the National Center for Law and Deafness (1992) estimated that "one out of every 100 people is profoundly deaf—unable to hear speech well enough to understand it" (1). However, not all of these individuals will use VRS, as they may not know sign language.

Simply being deaf does not make one an ideal user of VRS. Therefore, knowing the number of deaf people in the United States still does not provide a clear picture of who is using VRS. Not every deaf person uses sign language, nor is fluent enough in sign language to benefit from this form of telephone service. (Fluency is not a prerequisite for getting the equipment necessary to use VRS from their home or office—this is a fact that complicates the work of sign language interpreters, especially recent Interpreter Preparation Program graduates.)

I have heard that the number of people who have videophones is a small fraction of those who could use them. The reasons for this are tied to geography and employment of deaf people. First, simply having the equipment is not enough to have access. A person must also have high-speed Internet service, which, although more common now, is still an expense. Historically, deaf people have been largely under- and unemployed (National Center for Law and Deafness 1992). While many laws have been enacted to combat this situation, deaf people are still experiencing the effects of years of oppression that led to under- and unemployment. Second, more rural areas may not have the infrastructure to support the frames per second ideal to make the service effective.[17]

THE MAKING OF PUBLIC LIVES

Large portions of the lives of deaf persons, as with most individuals who have "spoiled identities" (Goffman 1963a), are public. Deaf people who rely on an interpreter to conduct even the most mundane interactions with non-deaf people are guaranteed very little, if any, privacy. There is always at least one other person present who presumably has nothing to gain from the outcome of an encounter. Even the most conscientious interpreter who maintains the confidentiality of those for whom she interprets, by her mere presence, is still making the lives of deaf people public.

Often public space is conceptualized as those areas where people may enter and exit freely. According to Lofland (1989) "the public realm is made up of the public places or spaces in a city, which spaces tend to be inhabited by persons who are strangers to one another or who 'know' one another only in terms of occupational or other non-personal identity categories such as bus driver/customer" (454). People pass each other on the street they share as they both make their way to their respective jobs; a customer enters a grocery store and engages the sales clerk about the freshness of the produce. Either way, people's engagement in public space is limited and often outcome-driven.

Those who occupy public spaces are bound by public-space norms. This is not to suggest that the "public realm is more rule-bound than other areas of social life" (Lofland 1998, 27). My point is only that they exist. These norms range from dress to behavior. That is, while there are no formal sanctions, in the United States, for someone wearing his pajamas in public, he may receive a raised eyebrow of disapproval for doing so. Similarly, while a person would not be sanctioned for reading a book in public, she would most definitely face sanctions for choosing to pick her nose in the same public space. A less extreme example is the use of

17. *Frames per second* refers to the speed at which images refresh themselves. The slower the frames per second, the more likely it is that the person signing may look stilted or even pixelated.

telephones. While it is becoming more acceptable for two or more individuals to occupy a common space and all to be on the phone talking to someone not in that space, it is considered a rude practice by most (Cox 2007). The success of a given interaction is based on the people's recognition and understanding of the rules that govern behavior.

Furthermore, public space is also constructed as an ableist space. When one must engage in a public sphere there is an assumption that one moves without assistance, mechanical or otherwise, and is able to see and hear. Although legislation such as the ADA has done much in the way of creating accessible spaces, the fact that there is legislation that mandates the alteration of space (or pathways to the space), through ramps or alternative information formats such as Braille, reinforces that public space is truly public only if one is not currently disabled.

The practices that govern occupants in public space are also based on ableist norms. Examples of these practices include standing when meeting a person or not tapping on a table to get the attention of a waiter. The former example obviously depends on the ability to stand. The latter is a common practice for deaf people, and the prohibition against it assumes that every person can articulate, in English, "Excuse me" to the waiter.

The telephone can form a bridge that connects people in these spaces—private to private or private to public. For many, there is an assumption that things discussed over the telephone are known only to the sender and the intended receiver of the message. However, some people must rely on a third person when attempting to communicate over the phone. Through the work of a variety of people, including deaf people, VRS connects deaf people with non-deaf, nonsigning people.

VRS is necessitated by a world that is structured for non-deaf people. Ableism, and, more specifically, audism (see Lane 1999), simultaneously oppresses deaf people while creating opportunities for individuals to capitalize on alleviating that oppression. Without deaf people as their consumers, VRS providers such as Ease Communication would not remain in business. One of the stated goals of both forms of relay (text and video) is to provide "functionally equivalent" telephone services; therefore, this book would have been incomplete had deaf users of the service not had a forum in which to discuss their experiences with VRS. This chapter presents some of these perspectives.

VRS allows deaf people who use sign language, rather than rely solely on lipreading, hearing aids, and/or cochlear implants, to have greater access to the world they live in via the telephone. Using this new service, deaf people can communicate in a visual, rather than a "vocal-auditory" (Baker-Shenk and Cokely 1980), language to converse with friends and family and attend to business over the phone. However, this new technology comes with old problems. These problems are a direct result of deaf people's reliance on a third party to communicate.

The chapter presents data gathered during focus groups with deaf people. The focus groups were conducted in two separate cities, in ASL, and were videotaped and then transcribed. The participants discussed a variety of experiences with both video and text relay services. The bulk of this chapter focuses on the data about VRS; however, to provide the context for this data I include the participants' comments about text relay as well. The discussions in the focus groups ranged from reasons for using VRS to the skills of interpreters. It should be noted that because the focus group discussions occurred in ASL, the quotations are my translations of the comments signed by the participants.

TEXT RELAY VERSUS VRS

During the focus groups, deaf people talked about a variety of issues they experience while using VRSs. Three issues seemed to be significant: text relay versus VRS; the skills of the interpreter, which may lead to misunderstandings; and the work that deaf people have to do while using VRS that can be complicated by the interpreter.

Establishing the Text Relay Service

The FCC, created by the Communication Act of 1934, is responsible for regulating interstate and international communications by radio, television, wire, satellite, and cable. Congress, via the ADA, ordered the FCC to make services for people with disabilities functionally equivalent to those of people without disabilities. The first attempt by the FCC to make the telephone accessible to people who were deaf or hard of hearing—the text relay service—occurred in 1992.

Agencies run by and for deaf people in California had organized to provide telephone services to deaf and hard of hearing people in the early 1980s. These agencies, relying on non-deaf operators to read messages from a teletype, were the first communication assistants or relay operators. However, these services were dependent on volunteers and "in 1985 the California Association of the Deaf (CAD) and the Greater Los Angeles Association of the Deaf (GLAD), an agency providing social services to deaf people, petitioned the California Utilities Commission to provide telephone access to deaf and hard of hearing residents of the state" (Padden and Humphries 2005, 118). The funded service started two years later.

While the text relay service was started by and for deaf people, it still required most of its users to communicate in their second language, English. Individuals who had become deaf later in life, or who were hard of hearing or fluent in English, communicated more successfully over this new service. Those people whose first language was ASL, although they had telephone access through the text relay service, still struggled to communicate freely. This is because ASL and English are not interchangeable. "According to the common misconceptions about ASL, it is either a collection of individual gestures or a code on the hands for spoken English" (Padden and Humphries 1988, 7). It is neither. "Although ASL does use gestures, as English uses sound, it is not made up merely of gestures any more than English is made up merely of sound. Individual signs are themselves structured grammatical units, which are placed in slots within sentences according to grammatical rules" (Padden and Humphries 1988, 7). Creating a medium by which deaf people type their message on a teletypewriter for the deaf (TTY)[18] to a third person, a communication assistant (CA), who then reads (relays) that message aloud to a non-deaf person and who also types the spoken message back from the non-deaf person to the deaf person, may have seemed logical and perhaps even ingenious. But it relies on the misleading premise discussed above.

Regulating Text Relay: A Model for VRS

Paragraph 64.604(a)(1) of the Mandatory Minimum Standards established by the FCC states:

[Telecommunication Relay Service] providers are responsible for requiring that [communication assistants] be sufficiently trained to effectively meet the specialized communications needs of individuals with hearing and speech disabilities; and that [communication assistants]

18. Another name for this device is a telecommunication device for the Deaf (TDD).

have competent skills in typing, grammar, spelling, interpretation of typewritten [American Sign Language], and familiarity with hearing and speech disability cultures, languages and etiquette.

However, although there are CAs who have some training in the grammatical structure of ASL in the text-relay service centers and are available to do sight translations of deaf people's English, these individuals have to be requested by either one of the callers or the initial CA. I have worked in two text-relay centers and received numerous calls from deaf friends and clients through the text relay. Often, the CA reads the message verbatim without consideration for linguistic or cultural differences. "Throughout the conversation, the operator maintains as strict a mediator role as possible: no personal conversations should take place between the operator and the deaf caller, nor should the operator engage in overmediation and try to respond on behalf of either party" (Padden and Humphries 2005, 119). And because the CA is not allowed to provide clarification, a sentence read verbatim could potentially create a miscommunication. In figure 3.1, I provide examples of what the CA might see on her or his screen and read verbatim, with a *possible* English equivalent in the right column. Only those words in all capital letters would be typed and then read to the person without a TTY. Without knowing the context, it is nearly impossible to be sure of intention.

While the first example, "MOTHER FATHER DEAF YOU Q," may be understood by someone who does not know ASL, the other examples may present more of a challenge and could lead to misunderstandings. Problems may also occur when the deaf person is trying to type in English. In the

ASL Written Form	Possible Intention
1 MOTHER FATHER DEAF YOU Q.	Are your parents deaf?
2 BOOK GIVE FINISH Q.	a Did you give them the book already? b Have you given me the book? c Did you give her the book?
3 SEE BLUE CAR Q THAT.	The car that I am talking about is that blue one.
4 BOBBY HIS.	That is just the way Bobby is.

FIGURE 3.1. *Examples of written ASL and the CA's possible interpretations.*

second example it is impossible to know the intent of the person talking without seeing the indexing (pointing) that would occur while signing. Since there are at least three possible meanings of the sent message, the receiver must either know the context or see the person sending the message so his intentions are clear. The third and fourth examples require more in-depth understanding of the language and culture of deaf people. Without this knowledge, the nonsigning person who hears these messages might be unable to decipher them. Often, when I get calls through the text relay, when the CA relays a statement that seems unclear I have to pause and sign the statement to myself so that I am able to understand it. I have heard that many people who can sign adopt this same practice. This should be understood as a shortcoming of this relay system, not of the communication abilities of deaf people who use the service.

A friend told me of another example that was typed by a deaf person: "I WANT YOU OBEY TO ME THAT IF CAN BUY TICKET." Here the caller is attempting to buy a ticket. The signs for OBEY and INFORM are almost identical; the difference is contextual and minute. Therefore, the caller's request to be "informed if he could buy a ticket" becomes confusing.

The fact that many people have very little experience with deaf people or ASL and therefore consider ASL a visual form of English contributes to these confusions. It is unclear from the literature whether the issue of language barrier was discussed when the TTY was devised. Despite its flaws, given the time and the technology available, the text-relay service was a tremendous step forward in terms of telephone access for deaf and hard of hearing people.

Video Relay Service: The Use of a Visual Language

In February of 2000, the FCC expanded the definition of *relay service* to include video relay service.[19] Video relay allows deaf people to rely on their native language—ASL—rather than on their second language—English—and communicate more freely. Jimmy, a deaf man who is a steward for the local postal union, sees video relay as providing a greater level of access than text relay does:

---

19. *Telecommunications Relay Services for Individuals with Hearing and Speech Disabilities*, Report and Order and Further Notice of Proposed Rulemaking, CC Docket No. 98-67, 15 FCC Rcd 5140, 5148-51 (2000) (*Improved TRS Order*).

With VRS, I feel like deaf people are finally equal to non-deaf people. The communication is smoother. I think that hearing people feel more comfortable communicating with us and are more likely to hire us too.

VRS provides deaf people greater freedom and control over when and how they conduct their everyday business over the phone. Jimmy's comment also refers to the assumptions non-deaf people make about deaf people when their first impression of a deaf person is based on a phone call. Some CAs in text relay do not make cultural or linguistic adjustments when reading the message from the deaf person; therefore, the message can sound robotic. Jimmy feels that the impression non-deaf people develop when their first experience is based on an interpreted, rather than read, interaction provided by a person trained in both languages and cultures is more flattering.

Edward, a deaf man in his eighties whose wife, children, and grandchildren are all deaf, also commented on the benefits of being able to communicate in his first language—ASL—and how there were miscommunications when he used the text relay:

> When I would call through the text relay, there were always misunderstandings. Now, I can use VRS and I can use my own language—ASL—and there are no misunderstandings.

One deaf individual, Deb, whose parents, husband, and children are also deaf, works for an agency that provides various services to deaf and hard of hearing people. She compared using video relay and text relay while she carries out the duties of her job:

> Like I said before, I call people through VRS at work. If I call a new customer or a business, I use VRS. It makes it easier to explain about policies and negotiate fees. Trying to conduct that same business over the TTY is really difficult. Because my English is not perfect, it is hard to find the right word to type on the TTY. I don't have to worry about that when I use VRS.

Deb's ability to communicate in her first language, ASL, allows her to focus on the purpose of her call. She does not have to worry about misunderstandings that are a result of her English.

Although both Deb and Edward say they are able to use their "own language" and that there were misunderstandings when they used the text relay, as discussions continued it became clear that this does not mean that there are no misunderstandings with VRSs. However, the misunderstandings are not a result of deaf people using their second language, but because of interpreters' errors.

MISUNDERSTANDINGS IN VRS

Although deaf people are able to use their native language with VRS, there are still misunderstandings. These misunderstandings occur for a variety of reasons. The most commonly cited misunderstanding arises from the inability of signed language interpreters to understand finger-spelled words. *Fingerspelling* refers to the practice of using different hand shapes, in the United States and parts of Canada, to represent the alphabet and numbers of spoken English. Here, Deb expresses her frustrations with signed language interpreters' inability to understand fingerspelling.

> One thing that is really frustrating is that interpreters don't understand fingerspelling. I notice the most problems with something like 6 or 16. Interpreters struggle with trying to understand which number I am signing. I think interpreters need a lot more training on numbers. One time I called an interpreter. I asked them if they would accept a last-minute request. I asked the interpreter and they accepted. I told them to add $6 per hour to their invoice and when I received their invoice they had added $16 per hour. Obviously the interpreter in video relay misinterpreted what I said. That is a problem I had with video relay.

One way to sign numbers 16 through 19 is to sign numbers 6 through 9 and simply shake the wrist.[20] On a two-dimensional screen it is sometimes difficult to catch the correct number. Even without the added factor of two dimensions, interpreters have expressed "frustration in reading fingerspelling and numbers" (Seal 2006, 6). I know from experience as an interpreter trainer and evaluator that interpreters struggle with understanding fingerspelling outside of video relay settings as well. This struggle is complicated when the interpreter must comprehend a language that relies on a particular space, the "area from the top of the head to just below the waist" (Greene and Dicker 1990, 20). When this two-dimensional

20. Another variation is to start with the number 10 and then twist the hand and end in, for example, 6 for 16.

space is viewed on a thirty-two-inch screen (sometimes smaller), the signing space becomes truncated.

Deb was attempting to find an interpreter for a last-minute request, which interpreters usually bill at a higher rate. Having the coordinator of interpreting services tell you that they are going to pay you $16 above your normal rate per hour for a last-minute job is out of the ordinary; however, given the shortage of interpreters that agencies have experienced and which some suggest is a result of the VRS industry, sign language interpreters are a sought-after resource and thus a bidding war, if you will, occurs (Bailey 2005). Interpreters themselves are cashing in on it too. Deb does not allow for the possibility that the video relay interpreter provided the correct interpretation but the sign language interpreter heard or wrote down the wrong number. Instead, Deb immediately blames the video relay interpreter.

Upon seeing Deb's comment, Edward suggested that perhaps it is not the fault of interpreters but of deaf people that misunderstandings occur:

> Well, we really should be clearer. Signing 16 (shaking the 6) instead of starting with the 10 then adding 6 is not clear. I don't know if we can really blame the interpreters when we are not clear.

Edward suggests that Deb's way of signing 16, shaking the 6 instead of showing 10 and then 6 may not be the clearest way to convey that number. Although he initially defends the interpreters, as he explains his own experiences he admits that he too has noticed that interpreters struggle with fingerspelling; however, he does not blame it on interpreting skill:

> Yeah, I really notice that people have problems with understanding fingerspelling or numbers. Many interpreters don't understand fingerspelling. I am not sure if they are not paying attention or what but they do have problems understanding fingerspelling.

Rather than suggest that interpreters need more training to improve their ability to understand fingerspelling, Edward suggests that they experience a momentary lapse in judgment, saying "perhaps they aren't paying attention." While Deb and Edward both discussed the issue of interpreters not understanding fingerspelling, neither of them defined the interpreters as "unqualified" because they were unable to read fingerspelling.

As stated before, deaf people's lives are lived out in public. Similarly, the work deaf people perform to use VRS is, in part, a product of the public milieu in which their calls occur. Here and elsewhere (see Brunson 2008, 2010), I refer to that work as "calculated consumer labor," to denote the mental and physical processes that go into this labor. Like all public space, there are rules that govern interactions between people. These rules promote civility and self-preservation. This work is both "emotional" (Cahill and Eggleston 1994; Hochschild 1979, 1983) and "face-work" (Goffman 1967). VRS makes the private lives of deaf people public and measures their actions against an ableist norm. As a marginalized group, deaf people perform various kinds of work as they attempt to gain access through VRS.

Different scholars have taken up the issue of emotional labor (see Steinberg and Figart 1999). However, a great deal of this examination takes as the starting point a paid employee and how they engage customers in such a way to make them more comfortable or less, depending on the purpose of the interaction. Cahill and Eggleston (1994) focus on the work people with disabilities perform to make nondisabled people they come in contact with more comfortable. It is this type of work that deaf people do when using VRS.

Although communication is easier with VRS, deaf people still discussed the many kinds of work they have to do when using VRS. This work is a product of the lack of qualified interpreters. Skill is a subjective measure and each deaf person may choose for his or her own reasons why the particular interpreter is not adequate (Brunson 2008). I asked Jake, a deaf man in his mid-thirties, what he did when he was making a call and the interpreter was less than qualified.

> I hang up and call back. I don't feel it is my responsibility to tell the interpreter or their supervisor that they aren't that good. I typically say something like, "Oh, I forgot the number so I will call back. Sorry about that." I know that it is unlikely that I will get the same interpreter again.

Even though Jake is pretending, he not only accepts the inconvenience of hanging up and perhaps having to wait for another interpreter to become available, but he also apologizes to the interpreter for any inconvenience he may have caused her. Jake was not the only person who accepted this burden. While talking to a colleague who is an interpreter for a VRS provider about this research and the work that deaf people do while using VRS, she recounted the practice that she and her husband, who is deaf, use when the interpreter is less than adequate:

> It happens a lot. My husband is not hard to understand. He uses American Sign Language and he is clear. He is also smart. I will sometimes call him several times a day. We have a code. When I start a sentence with "my sister" or "my cousin," he knows that the interpreter is not making any sense to me. He will then say, "Well, I have to go. My boss is coming." And we hang up and call back.

After I was told this story, I asked my colleague why she or her husband did not inform the interpreters that they were not being effective. She said, like so many others I spoke with, "It isn't worth my time." My colleague's statement that her husband is "not hard to understand" should be contextualized. It is not surprising that someone who spends a great deal of time with another person does not think that the person is hard to understand. This may not truly reflect the skill of the interpreter who is interpreting their call. Nevertheless, this story provides another example of the work taken up by callers when they feel their interpreters are not adequate.

In all of the cases, the callers weighed the time wasted in calling back with tolerating the interpreter's errors. Michael, a man who identifies as hard of hearing but is fluent in ASL, said:

> When the interpreter does not understand me, then, depending on the purpose of the call, I will just continue. For example, if I am calling my sister then I wouldn't worry about the interpreter making mistakes. However, if it was something important, I would tell the person I will call back and disconnect so that I can get another interpreter.

Some calls, according to Michael, are not worth going through the trouble of hanging up and calling back. B.T.M.H., a deaf man in his fifties, disagreed with Michael. B.T.M.H. felt that regardless of the purpose of the call, deaf people should hang up and call back:

> I disagree. I feel that regardless of the purpose of the call if the interpreter is not doing a good job then they should hang up and get another interpreter. They are professionals so they should be good. They get paid a lot of money, around $60,000, to do that job.

B.T.M.H.'s argument that interpreters are professionals who are paid well is an interesting one, given that he still does not address the issue of quality with the interpreter. Even though interpreters are professionals being paid very well, B.T.M.H. does not inform them of their errors. Nor does he contact their supervisor. None of the deaf people I spoke with contacted a supervisor to complain about the quality of the interpreter. When I asked them why they did not talk to a supervisor, people were unaware that that was an option for them. I then asked if they would talk to the supervisor now that they knew and the answer was still "no."

Asking for another interpreter or asking to speak to the supervisor appears to represent more than merely admonishing the service provider. It could also indicate something about the service recipient. In indicating that they are unsatisfied with the service they are receiving, deaf people might worry about showing they are frustrated. As Goffman (1967) suggests, "to appear flustered, in our society at least, is considered evidence of weakness, inferiority, low status, moral guilt, defeat, and other unenviable attributes" (102). To users of VRS, acknowledging that they are unhappy with the service they are being provided is also admitting that the service is needed; it might seem like they are admitting that they have less power than the interpreters who are there to provide them service.

Another possible reason for this approach taken by my informants is that the priority for them is completing their call. In situations when individuals, deaf and non-deaf alike, must confront poor service providers, the focus of the interaction changes. No longer is the focus on the services originally sought. Instead, the focus becomes the service delivery.

Aside from changing the focus of the interaction, there are other possible consequences to filing a complaint. Choosing to avoid confronting interpreters who may not be providing adequate service to the deaf caller points to the struggle that people with marginalized identities must face when filing a complaint. The amount of work required in filing a complaint goes beyond the actual telling of a problem; often it requires providing evidence, explaining why the behavior was problematic, and confronting the power differential that exists in society. Although not addressing the problem may save feelings, energy, and time for deaf callers, it also allows a system that may not be meeting the needs of those it is intended to serve to stay in place; the work of deaf people masks the quality of service they are receiving.

All of the deaf people I spoke with really liked VRS. They saw it as providing greater ease in telephone communication as compared to text relay. However, they also mentioned some drawbacks. The people in the focus groups did not describe these drawbacks in the language of work. However, their accounts, as clients, explained how they made the video relay system work for them.

For example, because of the small number of interpreters and high demand for the service, there are times when a deaf person may wait for several minutes before being connected to a interpreter and able to make a call. Since calls are placed in a queue and interpreters cannot pick and choose which calls they will take, deaf people must wait until another interpreter becomes available. This is typically a problem during "peak hours," when most people are placing calls. Some VRS providers try to counter the rush of calls during peak hours by educating deaf people about the best times to call so they will not encounter long wait times. This is probably most successful when the calls being made are of a personal nature. When calls are of a professional nature, however, it is more difficult. Deaf persons needing to conduct business with their financial institutions, for example, must do so between 9:00 A.M. and 5:00 P.M., when banks are open. These considerations mean that deaf people must schedule their calls strategically, thinking ahead about the best time to place a call and how long it might take, in ways that are not so necessary for hearing people who pick up the phone and dial the number they desire right away. This work of waiting for an interpreter, planning their phone calls, and determining the best time to call is not the only work that deaf people must do while using VRS; however, all of this work is calculated consumer labor. It is the work that deaf people are required to do in order to take advantage of VRS.

Previously, we learned that Edward placed the onus on deaf people for communication problems. Edward sees accepting responsibility for miscommunications as part of the work of communicating through a third person. Jimmy agreed with Edward, explaining that deaf people should double-check to make sure their messages are being understood:

> I think that deaf people should double check if the interpreter understands the message. We should ask to make sure that the interpreter knows that it is 6 and not 16. The deaf person is still responsible to make sure the message is clear.

Focusing solely on conducting their business on the phone, deaf people must also, according to Jimmy, "be responsible" for the accuracy of the interpretation, as well. As an interpreter, it has been my experience that when all of the people involved work together, the communication is much more successful. However, we must remember that the history of oppression deaf people have experienced has situated them in a vulnerable position. Even the most erudite deaf consumer still has very little control over the accuracy of an interpretation. Their ability to double-check meanings depends on several factors. Above all, it depends on the deaf person's willingness to ask for clarification from the interpreter and the interpreter's willingness to provide that clarification.

This is not solely the result of deaf people not wanting to confront interpreters. The accounting mechanism in place for VRS does not make space for documenting the work of deaf people as they attempt to gain access. Within the official record of VRS, deaf peoples' work remains invisible. What gets counted are the minutes the interpreters are connected to the deaf callers, not whether the deaf callers are satisfied with the services they receive.

CONCLUSION

VRS is intended to provide greater functional equivalency for deaf people on the telephone. As the focus group participants compared video relay with text relay, it was obvious that they preferred VRS. However, there is room for improvement.

Our interactions are organized, in part, by the spaces in which they occur. Even though spaces that are designated as public are said to be open to everyone, there are rules that govern interactions that occur within them. These rules represent shared expectations and are intended to minimize social collisions. However, these rules are also based on able-bodied norms. VRS centers are spaces designed for the benefit of deaf people that make deaf people's lives public and hold them to the norms of public intercourse.

The deaf people I spoke with had a great appreciation for VRS. They saw it as providing more equal access for them on the telephone, because they are able to use their first language rather than English to communicate with others. However, deaf people still must work to gain access through VRS.

As a population that is disabled and patronized by society, deaf people have developed strategies that aid in dealing with service providers. These strategies are intended to get their needs met while avoiding possibly upsetting interpreters. While this is emotional work, it is also empowering work. It is empowering work because deaf people are taking control over their calls and their lives. The people I spoke with did not seem to resent the fact that they were performing this work. In fact, they saw it as a necessary component of gaining access.

However, it also indicates the disempowered position deaf people occupy in society. Deaf people are made to feel, directly or indirectly, by interpreters and society, that they are not entitled to demand access. They are reminded daily that their needs are secondary to those of the non-disabled person who is assisting them. Furthermore, complaints by deaf people may mark them as ungrateful.

When talking about their experiences, users of VRS did not acknowledge that they were performing this emotional and invisible work. I suspect this is a product of an inaccessible society, one that constantly reminds deaf people that they are dependent on the kindness of others. Also, if deaf people were to upset the service providers, they might run the risk of losing access altogether. Schein (1992) found that deaf students in Alberta, Canada, were reluctant to complain about interpreters because they feared the interpreters would stop providing services for them and they would be left without access to their classes. While there are no data on whether interpreters retaliate against deaf people who complain about the services they are provided, the following joke told in the Deaf community illustrates that trust is at least a consideration for deaf people:

> A sheriff asks [a deaf] man where the stolen money is hidden. The deaf man signs and the interpreter voices, "He says, he does not know what you are talking about."
>
> After half an hour of continual denials by the deaf man, the exasperated sheriff places a gun against the deaf man's head and says, "If you don't tell me where the money is hidden, I will kill you."
>
> The interpreter signs the threat, and the now-terrified deaf man responds, "I hid it under the back stairs at my cousin's house."
>
> The sheriff, sensing that something has changed in the deaf man's persistent denials, eagerly asks, "What did he say?" Quickly, the interpreter answers, "He says he's not afraid to die." (cited in Stewart, Schein, and Cartwright 1998, 87)

Even though this joke does not directly address an interpreter outright denying a deaf person access, it does address the underlying issue of trust in the interpreter to do the right thing.

The skill of sign language interpreters is an issue for users of VRS. Even though, as Jimmy said, he feels that VRS is more "equal to non-deaf," there are strategies that deaf people have to employ to ensure they get access. Whether they are being vigilant about fingerspelling clarity or devising stories so they can hang up without telling the interpreter that they are not performing successfully, it is obvious that deaf people are engaging in a lot of work to accommodate differences in the interpreters' skills. This is work that non-deaf people do not engage in while they are placing calls.

It would be easy, and perhaps tempting, to place the blame for misunderstandings or for the additional work deaf people must do while using VRS solely on interpreters. However, the reality is that interpreters are the front-line workers in a large system that spans beyond a single interpreter. The next two chapters investigate the organization of that large system, looking first at the daily work of interpreters and then at the systems used for monitoring their work.

Chapter 4

"We're Providing Access"

All of the work, invisible and visible, discussed by the deaf people in chapter 3 is intricately linked to the sign language interpreter whose cubicle their call is dropped into. Sign language interpreters are people fluent in one or more forms of sign languages and a spoken language. They have learned, through formal training or life experiences, to "take meaning in one language and fully express that meaning accurately in the second language" (Neumann Solow 2000, 1). Considering culture, class, gender, sexuality, race, and a whole host of other factors that influence interactions between two people, sign language interpreters aim, ideally, for each person to be understood while the interpreter remains objective.

Definitions of a good sign language interpreter vary from person to person and are dependent on the particular needs of those involved (see Brunson 2008). Each deaf person has her or his affinities for particular interpreters and thus it is difficult to attempt to define what skills a "good" interpreter possesses. As with any art, a patron's appreciation depends greatly on their own preferences and experiences.

While it is difficult to define a "good" interpreter, some standard, albeit vague, must be used to monitor the provision of video relay services. It is through this standardization that access can be measured. The Telecommunication Relay Service rules define a qualified interpreter as "an interpreter who is able to interpret effectively, accurately, and impartially, both receptively and expressively, using any specialized vocabulary" (47 C.F.R. § 64.601). Although the rules invoke the terms "effectively" and "accurately" there is no explanation of how this is determined.

In this chapter, I discuss, from the standpoint of sign language interpreters, the work they perform. This is what Dorothy Smith (2006) calls "work knowledge." There are two aspects to work knowledge: "One is a person's experience of and in their own work, what they do, how they do it, including what they think and feel; a second is the implicit or explicit coordination of his or her work with the work of others" (Smith 2006, 151).

Here, I use data gathered during twenty-one formal interviews and informal discussions with interpreters, unsolicited stories interpreters told me as they learned of my research, and my own experience as an interpreter to explore the VRS work of sign language interpreters.

THE WORK OF SIGN LANGUAGE INTERPRETING

Many people have seen a spoken language interpreter work. It is common to see someone translate Spanish or French into English on a television show. Because of the role the United States has in the global market, we often see diplomats, foreign and domestic, listening attentively as someone translates into their ear. While sign language interpreters and spoken language interpreters do perform similar functions in society, there are some differences.

Interpreters are charged with the task of assisting two or more people who do not share a language or culture to communicate. To successfully convey both cultural and linguistic features of one language into another language, interpreters must consider a whole host of sociolinguistic features (Cokely 1992). These features are a compilation of factors brought to bear on a given interaction by the participants, which includes the interpreter. They include the participant's fluency in the language of choice, mood, knowledge of subject matter, and several others. Even this incomplete list of factors that influence an interaction demonstrates that sign language interpreting, like all interpreting, is an embodied practice, which one interpreter referred to as "personal investment." Estelle, who has experienced interpreting in a variety of settings and learned the craft in church, likens sign language interpreting work to that of an ambassador:

> I think the role of interpreters in general, not only by signed language interpreters, is greatly understated. I think interpreters are really, what I call, the grunts of building cultural understanding. If it wasn't for those small little interactions that interpreters help facilitate between two sets of people or two individuals who come from different experiences we [as a society] would be just so separate. So for me and my view and also with a little more [knowledge about] spoken language interpreters and the challenges they face, how they do what they do and how they got to where they're at, it has just become more evident to me that fundamentally, at its core, the importance of interpreters

is just as a cultural bridge. For those who, I think, either don't have that understanding or lose sight of it, there is a piece when we are actually doing the work of interpreting, when we are facilitating the communication between these two different languages, I think, a big part ends up missing in, sort of, the translation or interpreting between two languages, not only between the two people we are facilitating communication between but for ourselves as well. Because there is a high degree of personal investment in the work we do; whether it is signed or spoken language, it is a personal investment. Unless we see our role in a bigger way than just that one little exchange in, "how do I say this word in that language and how do I say that word in this language?" I think we lose out on a bigger piece.

Even though Estelle refers to us as the "grunts," she obviously considers sign language interpreters' work to be very important. She considers it the practice of bringing together two or more people who do not share a language or culture. She also warns that the practice of merely finding a sign for every word and vice versa, rather than examining every utterance for its implicit and explicit meaning, is not an effective practice. Furthermore, Estelle recognizes that communication is an important component of any society. This suggests that she sees that interpreters are not merely helping two people communicate, but are, in effect, strengthening our society.

REASONS FOR DOING VRS WORK

There is no denying that video relay service work is different than the practice of interpreting in face-to-face settings. The mechanism by which the interpreting is initiated (e.g., computer equipment and programs) is not the only distinguishing feature of VRS work; the relationship between the deaf consumer and access to localized information is also different. For example, in face-to-face interactions interpreters are members of the same geographic community as the deaf person for whom they are interpreting. Street names, local events, and even other deaf people are known to the interpreter, and therefore some of the context necessary to produce an effective interpretation is already known. This often makes interpreters' work easier. Why then, would interpreters choose to work in VRS centers? I believe that most interpreters want to provide communication access; however, when I asked participants why they wanted to do VRS work, the answers focused on three primary motivations: financial motives, skill enhancement, and working with a different consumer pool.

Financial Motives: The Royal Treatment

It is unrealistic to believe interpreters do their jobs without expectation of payment. Interpreting can be a career. Therefore, when people mentioned money as a motivation for interpreting for VRS, I was not surprised. One interpreter, D. Vahded, spoke about the lifestyle he experienced during the initial months VRS was in operation:

> [It was] the novelty of it. [They were] flying me to [another city] and [I was] staying in a hotel. Brian put it best. He said, "It's like camp." You get away for a little bit and you do some work. Of course, I was working fourteen-hour days, I would work seven hours in the morning and seven hours at night and I would have the day to lounge around and do nothing but watch TV and eat, and I would get reimbursed for it. As an interpreter you don't get a whole hell of a lot of opportunities to travel [like that].

In the beginning, VRS providers did not have centers in every state. As more deaf people received videophones, providers had to train more interpreters. To do this, Ease Communication would fly interpreters from various locations to a central place to be trained. These trips were completely paid for by Ease Communication. Interpreters stayed at hotels and were reimbursed for food and other expenses. They were also shuttled back and forth to the call center.

When VRS first started, at least in the two cities where this study occurred, interpreters were earning approximately $30 an hour for face-to-face interpreting if they were considered to be "fully certified," meaning that they held either the Comprehensive Skills Certificate or both the Certificate of Transliteration and Certificate of Interpretation from the Registry of Interpreters for the Deaf (see Appendix A for description). Most of the interpreters I spoke with mentioned that Ease Communication paid more than what they were used to earning. The same interpreter who could earn $30 an hour for face-to-face interpreting could earn nearly $10 more per hour for work in VRS centers.

Just like D. Vahded, Margaret, an interpreter and director of one of the centers, enjoyed the royal treatment she received from Ease Communication. She also liked the amount of money they paid: "The money is good, they are going to pay for me to fly out, pay for the hotel and they are going to pay me a really great weekend check. . . . Rock on, I am there!" Theodore also agreed that the money made the decision to work for Ease Communication easy: "I have a wife and a baby. I had to pay the bills. They paid the most. It was plain and simple. They paid the most."

Many of the interpreters I spoke with did not work solely for Ease Communication. Even those who were on staff and worked approximately twenty-nine hours a week still held jobs at other locations. In some cases, this employment was teaching interpreting or sign language at the local junior college; a few worked at the local university as staff interpreters; in most cases, the interpreters also worked as freelance interpreters providing interpreting in medical, legal, and business arenas. A few of the interpreters had their own interpreting referral agencies and have freelance and staff interpreters who reported to them. In addition to working at Ease Communication and doing freelance interpreting, many of the interpreters were also parents or in a committed relationship with someone they lived with. Undoubtedly, maintaining their relationships and parenting children also consumed a great deal of their time and energy. VRS provides an opportunity for interpreters to work a set number of hours that may change only slightly from week to week.

Although many of the interpreters I spoke with worked for Ease Communication up to twenty-nine hours a week and still did considerable freelance work, they did mention another monetary consideration. VRS centers provide a single location where interpreters go, which reduces the number of other jobs and locations they have to drive to during the day, and cuts down on the amount of money spent on gas on a weekly basis.

Skill Enhancement: Sign-to-Voice Practice

Every interpreter has her or his strengths. Interpreting from ASL into English seems to create an increased anxiety in some interpreters, however. Humphrey and Alcorn (1994) suggest this anxiety is unfounded for the properly trained interpreter:

Some people contend that sign-to-voice interpreting is the harder part of the process, since reading signs is more challenging than producing signs. This is a common misperception. Actually, if one's second language is acquired in an appropriate manner, s/he should be much stronger working from her/his second language into her/his native language. (196)

There are factors other than whether a person has acquired a second language in an "appropriate manner," however. Neumann Solow (2000) points out that working from ASL into English is no more difficult than working from English to ASL. That is, the process of interpreting is the same in both situations. What do differ, according to Neumann Solow, are the expectations on the interpreter. Deaf and non-deaf people's exposure to interpreters influences what they expect to get from the interpreter and his interpretation. In other words, how much work the recipient of an interpretation is willing to put forth depends on how much experience she has with interpreters, her understanding of the processes, and a whole host of other variables.

Neumann Solow (2000) suggests that to improve one's ability in working from ASL to English (and perhaps to reduce anxiety), interpreters need to gain more experience doing it. This does not simply mean socializing with ASL users. But where can this practice occur? Unfortunately, many deaf people are disproportionately under- and unemployed (Blanchfield et al. 2001; Macleod-Gallinger 1992). Until recently, there has not been a significant number of deaf people in positions of authority who rely on interpreters. Thus, typically, interpreters are working from a spoken language (e.g., English) to a signed language. They interpret in locations such as classrooms, courtrooms, and business meetings, and in other situations where deaf people do not have the opportunity to make comments. This unidirectional flow of information does not allow for interpreters to develop skill in going from sign language to spoken language. That was the case for Diane, who started her career working in K–12 educational settings with children:

> I worked in elementary K–12. I did that and then later I did freelance educational interpreting until I felt comfortable enough to work with adults. A lot of the kids [I worked with] were oral or [signed] English. I was fluent enough that my [English to American Sign Language] was no problem. My fear was going from American Sign Language to English. The receptive [work] was my fear.

The lack of employment opportunities for deaf people has had a circular effect. Since deaf people typically do not hold positions in which they run meetings or provide presentations to non-deaf audiences, interpreters have had limited opportunities to improve their skill providing sign-language-to-English interpretation, which, in turn, means they struggle when called upon to provide such interpretations. Interpreters have therefore had to seek out opportunities where they can practice and perfect this craft, which unfortunately often means that practice occurs in real-life situations.

Interpreters mentioned improving their sign-to-spoken language skill as a motivating factor for doing VRS work. As a setting in which an interpreter can work with over fifteen different people in a shift; and where information is typically presented both to and from the deaf caller, VRS provides an optimal, albeit not ideal, situation to practice interpreting from sign language to English. Margaret also mentioned both the novelty of VRS and the ability to improve interpreters' skills in interpreting from sign language to spoken language as another motivating factor for her going to work at a VRS center:

> It is something new. It's something big. Video relay interpreter service work is paramount in helping [an] "ok" interpreter become really great because the amount of exposure that you get, the amount of voicing opportunities you have . . . for me, I was really excited. [Interpreting in a] classroom [where the] rigor often goes one way [from the teacher to the student]. Someone is talking at you and you produce [in ASL] this great piece of text. But it doesn't often go in the other way [from student to teacher]. So you have to seek out opportunities to improve in that area. They usually don't walk to your door and [knock] and say, "hi, can someone voice for me?" That is something that I really enjoy doing so I wanted to push that threshold. Why not?

As Margaret mentions, interpreters must seek out those opportunities to improve their ability to convey deaf people's ideas in a spoken language. However, when I spoke to Amber, another interpreter and director, about the idea of practicing sign-to-spoken-language interpreting, she responded, "It really isn't practice. It is like landing a plane. You either do it or you don't. All you can do is hope that you do it well." Amber's comment demonstrates that she sees video relay as a place where you are actually doing the interpreting. While some may consider it an ideal place for practicing interpreting from a sign language to a spoken language, Amber does not believe VRS is the place interpreters should be getting their practice in sign-to-spoken-language skills.

Consumer Pool: I Want to Go Where Nobody Knows My Name

In addition to the financial and skill enhancement incentives, two interpreters I spoke with also considered the prospect of interpreting for people outside of their city and state an important reason for working in video relay. Kathryn, whose parents are deaf and who is married to a deaf man, sees VRS as an opportunity to interpret for people who do not know her or her family:

> When I interpret [locally] people know me. They know my family. Some people don't like having me interpret for them because they are afraid that I am going to tell my parents. I can't tell you how many times I have been told, by a deaf person, "Don't forget you can't tell your parents that you interpreted for me." They will then turn around and tell me to tell my parents "Hello" for them. They can't have it both ways.

Our work is fraught with contradictions, a fact that will become more pronounced given our aspirations of attaining professional status (Brunson 2006). Interpreters must interact with deaf people so that they can maintain their skills and become known to the Deaf community but must simultaneously appear not to socialize with any deaf people to avoid being seen as violating their confidence with other Deaf community members. Similarly, deaf people will often praise and even seek out the children of deaf parents to be their interpreters but will also fear that the interpreter with deaf parents is too involved with the Deaf community and therefore cannot be trusted to keep information private. Kathryn has chosen to work in VRS so as to avoid the "praise and scrutiny" she experiences in her local community.

Another interpreter, Tyler, who does not have deaf parents, has also chosen to work in VRS to avoid members of the local Deaf community. Tyler is in the middle of changing careers. He is planning on becoming a different type of service provider in the same Deaf community in which he has been interpreting. He sees VRS as a means to distance himself so that he can change perceptions of his role within the Deaf community:

> Once I graduate, I want to work in this community. Up until now, people here have only known me as an interpreter. I don't want them to see me that way anymore. I think if I work in video relay then I can interpret for people I don't know and that will get me out of this community until I graduate.

Tyler has worked for several years developing a reputation as an interpreter. In this capacity, he could not have an opinion or provide counsel to people for whom he was interpreting. In his new capacity as a counselor, he will assume a more authoritative role in people's lives. To do that successfully, he wants to distance himself from being seen as an interpreter. For both Kathryn and Tyler, their desire to avoid deaf people who live in their communities means they will attempt to not accept calls from people they know.

DOING THE WORK DIFFERENTLY: THE IMPORTANCE OF CONTEXT

Anonymity is not the only reason that interpreters may choose to not accept a call from a particular caller. In some cases, the interpreter may not feel that she or he is qualified to interpret. Sarah, with over seventeen years of interpreting experience and two years of video relay experience, said, "I feel awful but it got really bad for me. There were times I would 'accidentally' disconnect from the caller so they would have to call back for another interpreter. I didn't do that often but in those situations that I didn't feel like I could do the work . . . especially in situations that I wouldn't do outside of video relay." While Sarah's actions are perhaps the extreme, it points to the importance for her to be able to decline a call when she is not comfortable. As Sarah continued, it appeared that she was usually uneasy because she did not have the context for the call.

In the last twenty years, the field of interpreting has gone through various changes, which are reflected in the scholarship that has been produced. One of the most notable texts on the work of sign language interpreters was written by Dennis Cokely in 1992. In *Interpreting: A Sociolinguistic Model,* Cokely says, "Setting, purpose, and participants are contextual factors or components that influence any communicative interaction" (23). This quote, and the study in which it appeared, argues that interpreters not only must be fluent in ASL and English but they must also examine the larger social context in which their work occurs. When they take the context into consideration, interpreters are more effective. Cokely's work in the sociolinguistics of interpreting has been read by interpreters in different interpreter training programs in the United States and abroad.

Earlier I quoted Estelle, who mentioned that interpreters need to begin "seeing our role in a bigger way than just that little exchange." This comment refers to the need to consider the context in which our interpreting occurs. It is not only the immediate context of a given situation but the larger social context as well. That is, interpreters must attempt to understand the purpose of the interaction and keep in mind that their performance influences not only the immediate interaction but also perceptions of sign language interpreting as a field. Since this may be the non-deaf person's first time interacting with a deaf person, interpreters can also influence that person's perception of deaf people in general. Therefore, interpreters should not only know about the purpose of a particular interaction but also about the people involved in the interaction. Sometimes to understand the context of a given exchange between two people, interpreters may want to talk with the callers and gather necessary information before the interpreting process begins. Although thirty seconds may seem like an adequate time to gather information that will help the interpreter, in face-to-face interpreting interpreters traditionally arrive at least fifteen minutes before an appointment to meet with both the deaf and non-deaf individuals so that everyone can become comfortable with each other's communication styles.

This is not always necessary, however. In some cases, the context is revealed when the call is placed. Often the setting can provide "contextual clues to the meaning of the message" (Stewart, Schein, and Cartwright 1998, 41). Interpreters' experiences inside and outside of VRS working and socializing with deaf people also help them develop "schemas or scripts" for various situations (Humphrey and Alcorn 1994). These scripts allow interpreters to use their closure skills when all of the information is not presented explicitly.

For example, when a deaf person wants to call T-Mobile, chances are the call is going to be about their Sidekick or other two-way paging device. Or when the deaf person is calling the Social Security office, they are likely going to be talking to someone about disability (or other governmental subsistence) benefits. Although they could also be calling T-Mobile to purchase a new phone or to call in sick to work, or calling the Social Security office because they are dealing with an ailing loved one and need to get some answers, they are definitely not calling T-Mobile to order a pizza or the Social Security office to make an appointment to have their teeth cleaned.

Some interpreters have decided to take a few seconds before the call begins to gather "necessary" information, although this is not a practice shared by all interpreters. Elizabeth, an interpreter with more than eighteen years of experience, told me about a time when she tried to provide some of the background information to another interpreter who was going to help on a call. It was a 911 call, which is processed differently than a regular call. When placing a 911 call, there are additional steps required. Immediately, another interpreter must be called in to assist with the call, although she does not have to take over the call. In addition to the second interpreter, because the call can be originating in a state that is different from the VRS center, there are additional numbers to call so that the correct 911 dispatch office is contacted. Furthermore, the interpreter is supposed to stay on the line and provide the 911 operator the VRS center's phone number, not the deaf caller's videophone number. Here, Elizabeth recounts her interaction with the deaf caller and the assisting interpreter, Bernice:

> The caller said, "I need to call the landlord so we can call the police." I tried to clarify. I asked "Do you mean you want to call the police about your landlord?" The caller responded that she wanted to call the landlord and tell him that she wanted to call the police.
>
> Now, I know that you don't have to call the landlord if you want to call the police. You just call the police. But she didn't know. So I processed the call. We called the landlord and she told him that she was calling the police. The landlord was confused. He didn't know why this person was calling him. We hung up with the landlord and called the police. Now I have never done a 911 call before. Bernice was passing by so I grabbed her and said, "It is a 911 call and I don't know how to do it." She took over. I began to tell her what the call was about and she said, "I don't need know that." I was taken aback because I would want to know what the call was about. What is the situation? Is someone bleeding, dying, or what? But that is Bernice. She is really a machine-model type of interpreter.
>
> She started processing the call and was completely confused. If she would've let me tell her about the call, she would've understood what the call was about and probably would not have struggled. When the call was over, she looked at me and said, "Wow that was awkward." I said, "Well I tried to explain everything to you but you didn't need to know, right?" I thanked her and she left.

Initially, this looks as if Bernice is being uncooperative. While both interpreters are aware of the rules regarding efficiency, Elizabeth appears to take the additional time to ensure her colleague is able to effectively interpret the situation by providing her with information she feels is important. Even though neither mentions the fact that efficiency is calculated when both the non-deaf and deaf person are connected, the fact that

Bernice was uninterested in gathering information about the call demonstrates that she sees her role as a conduit rather than an ambassador, as Estelle considers it. While this practice of not gathering information is counter to the ethos of interpreting, it is indirectly supported by Ease Communication and the National Exchange Carrier Association through policies that count efficiency only after both callers are connected. Bernice is a staff interpreter while Elizabeth is a contract interpreter. It may be that Bernice feels more constrained by her staff position or more responsibility to adhere to the company's policies.

Staff interpreters, however, are not the only ones who would rather not have any of the background information. In fact, Theodore, a freelance interpreter, told me that he explains to callers that he does not want any of the background information before the call begins:

> Jeremy: Do you find that it goes smoother when you get some idea of what the call is about before the call begins?
>
> Theodore: I prefer not to ask. Yeah, because if I ask for that information then they start providing with me a lot of details that I don't want to remember. I always tell them to hold on if they start to provide me with information. I want them to hang on until I have placed their call and then they can do their thing.

There are times, however, when Theodore asks for clarifications before the call begins:

> The only time I ask about who they are calling or what the call is about is if there is bad lighting, poor picture quality, something like that. If I am having a difficult time understanding them, then I will try to get some additional information but if I can understand their signs clearly then I don't ask. I just don't want that.

It is not clear how Theodore is able assess his ability to understand the caller if he does not allow them to provide at least some information to him prior to the placing of the call.

> Jeremy: Why don't you want that information up front all the time?
>
> Theodore: Because if they give me that information then they often assume that I am going to take care of their call for them. I would rather them just hang on so that I can place the

call and interpret for them. It isn't my job to remember it and I know I won't remember it so let's not even get into that kind of a situation. I will just call, I don't tell people this, but I will interpret. I don't need their personal life story to do this job. Deaf people want to give you much more information than you really need and I don't want to get into that scenario. I just ask them to hold until I have placed the call and then they can say what they want.

Jeremy: How do people respond to you?

Theodore: Typically, I will sign "Hold on, because I am not going to remember." They don't have a problem with that. They will usually say, "Oh ok that is fine. No problem." At least that has been my experience.

Theodore sees the practice of getting the context as problematic because the deaf caller could then provide him with information that he does not want or need. Just like Bernice, Theodore avoids gathering any information before the callers are connected. Theodore's underlying reason is that he does not want to be held responsible for information. His concern is that once the non-deaf person is connected, the deaf caller will tell him to explain what he had just been told. However, when he is having difficulty understanding the caller he will gather information and not worry about the deaf person relying on him to negotiate on her or his behalf. What Theodore did not discuss with me is how he signs the questions to the deaf caller. It could be that deaf callers are giving Theodore "too much information" because they are not clear as to what information he needs or what information will help him interpret effectively.

In addition, getting the context can help interpreters provide an accurate interpretation. The irony is that Theodore is concerned about creating a situation in which deaf callers are dependent on him. However, by adhering to the conduit model in this situation, a model intended to maximize the deaf person's control and minimize the interpreter's influence, Theodore is demonstrating he, not the deaf caller, is in charge of how the process will work.

The relationship between sign language interpreters and the deaf people they work with is complex. Interpreters provide access in an attempt to empower but they are also often friends (or at least empathizers) with the deaf people with whom they work. Even though the codes of professional conduct endorsed by the national organization—the Registry of Interpreters for the Deaf (RID)—provide some guidance on how to interact with deaf people to ensure interpreters do not unduly influence the interaction they are interpreting, their mere presence changes the interactions that occur in a given situation.

D. Vahded states he is less invested while doing VRS work than he is when he does face-to-face interpreting; however, he still relies on context when interpreting. He uses cues that are occurring in the setting as inspiration for how he is going to interpret. He suggests that this practice helps facilitate communication and is less intrusive to the process. But his comments also point to the many gray areas, where interpreters may be unsure about how to proceed in this new context:

> One example is with VRS interpreting. It is about relaying emotion. Does the interpreter become an active participant in the conversation by way of representing the affect of the participants? Like if the deaf caller is crying, do you say, "oh the caller is crying?" Or say, "It appears that the caller is crying"? Or do you adopt that affect (mimicking crying). Because you are seeing them cry. Where is that boundary? That was never addressed in the ITP.

Emotions are not the only contextual feature that D. Vahded is unsure about. Another one is the vernacular that a caller might use:

> I put it out the same way, matching language, but I think with VRS I think it happens far more frequently that I am confounded with the "Do I . . ." 'cause as an interpreter you want to minimize your impact on the conversation. Well if you have two people from Detroit and they are speaking the urban colloquial register then I would be affecting that conversation more if I kept it in the "Hi, how are you today?" rather than say, "What's up?" That is why I have tended to interpret the way I have.

Interpreters are not interchangeable. It is impossible to have an interpreter who is able to accurately interpret both content and context for every situation. Some interpreters may, when faced with a situation that they are unfamiliar with, such as religious matters or OBGYN issues, work to provide an accurate, content-only interpretation. D. Vahded, on the other hand, chooses to attempt both:

> VRS interpreting has just come around since I finished the [Interpreting Training] Program so I am sure they are talking about it now. I could

probably go back and take classes now in it. (laughing). Those things I still struggle with. If I have a black caller and he is using (starts to rock body) his urban colloquial, and his counterpart is on the same level. Do I want to keep it white bread (signifies a higher level/register*)? Or do I want to bring it to that level (bring it down*)? What I have done is try to match. Recently, I had a colleague, Brenda, who was observing me, say that men tend to match the hearing person instead of matching the deaf person. I guess, when I am listening to the hearing person, I tend to match that level instead of the [deaf person's] register. I am not sure how I feel about that. It is a little unnerving. I am very aware of my involvement in the process. These are things that I have questions about and since I haven't gotten an answer, I go with my gut. My gut tells me to voice it as, (feigning a black dialect), "What up, whatcha fit'n do nite?" I am going to try to match that and relax a little with my signing. Make it clear but make it . . . in sync with what their conversation is.

During a Deaf People of Color conference, a discussion occurred about the (in)ability of interpreters to effectively interpret for people of color on VRS (Lightfoot 2007). One of the discussion points of that meeting was that interpreters should not assume they understand the context. Here, D. Vahded attempts to provide the context as well as the content. He also recognizes that these decisions may be questionable and would like to discuss them with other interpreters:

Wrong or right, that is how I do it. These are things that I would probably benefit from discussions with other interpreters on so that I can figure out how to handle these issues.

I would argue that this practice of making assumptions about a person's background and their communication style is a product of limited access with callers on VRS. Even though D. Vahded's behavior is most likely the extreme, interpreters are often left without enough information to provide an accurate interpretation of the caller's intent unless they inquire further before the call begins.

Sarah told me about a situation in which adhering to the policies that preclude her from gathering the context of the call caused her to struggle to provide an accurate interpretation:

* Indicates those comments that were signed and spoken simultaneously.

The caller came up on my screen. He was wearing a white turban kind of thing. I was searching for any kind of clue to what the context was. When the hearing person answered the phone, the caller spelled his name. I said to the hearing person, "Hi, it's Yamez." The hearing person started to repeat the name, "Yamez? Yamez?" I realized I had probably said it wrong. I started to place the emphasis on different syllables. I knew it was Yamez but I just didn't know how to say it. After what seemed like thirty minutes but was really just a really long minute, the hearing person said, "James, is that you?" I about died.

Sarah explained that once she was locked into the idea that James was of Middle Eastern descent because he was wearing a turban, even though she should have understood J-A-M-E-S when it was fingerspelled, she just knew it had to be pronounced "Yamez." Furthermore, she attributes this error to the practice of not getting the context of a call or being able to talk with the caller before the call begins. She said, "This story epitomizes the problem with VRS. They are trying to reduce us to robots and robots can't effectively interpret."

The stories that Sarah and D. Vahded told demonstrate the context that interpreters bring to a given setting. Without knowing the people that they are interpreting for, interpreters (who are human) end up making assumptions. These assumptions are based on their own experiences, prejudices, and biases. While these sometimes benefit one or both of the callers, they are often not accurate representations of the people for whom they are interpreting. They are actually manifestations of one's lack of knowledge and superficial interaction with the callers. This is different than when interpreters work in face-to-face situations. As D. Vahded explains in his comments about interpreting for a student at a local university,

You know that student. You have some interaction with *that* student. Now of course there isn't a lot of interaction from the student in terms of the information; [it] tends to flow one way, from the teacher to the students. There are occasions when the students have to give presentations, but you usually have the presentation before the date and you know what they are going to say. Also, in the educational setting your register is going to be up here (showing a high register*). You get more of an intelligent individual in that arena. You are going to be able to work in a register that is familiar, more comfortable, for me. Then

* Indicates those comments that were signed and spoken simultaneously.

again, given my history there are a lot of different registers that I am comfortable with. I can definitely thug it up if I need to.

Working in an educational setting is different than VRS interpreting but it is also different than most face-to-face interpreting. When working in an educational setting, the interpreter usually works with the same student for the entire semester (or year, in a K–12 setting). Therefore, an interpreter has the benefit of becoming much more familiar with the person for whom they are interpreting. Regardless of the differences between educational and other kinds of face-to-face interpreting, the context is typically provided before a job starts. In addition to knowing the context, interpreters are able to interact with the deaf person prior to the actual interpreting. Using the time before they begin to interpret, interpreters are able to assess a register appropriate for the situation and the consumers involved.

The uncertainty displayed in the stories presented above is also a product of the newness of VRS. Since there have been very few empirical studies about VRS, the training of interpreters has not been able to accommodate the new demands that are placed on them. Therefore, each interpreter must rely on her own experiences to provide interpretation. However, interpreters do not always have sufficient background in interpreting before taking VRS calls and therefore the cache of experience on which they can draw is rather limited. When I first applied at Ease Communication, in Arizona, the advertisement said that interpreters must hold a national certification from RID or the National Association of the Deaf and have over five years of interpreting experience. As of 2007, Ease Communication and other video relay providers advertise for "qualified" rather than "certified." The requirement for "qualified" allows for a more subjective measurement. Each company can determine what constitutes a qualified interpreter rather than rely on a national certification awarded by RID. Some interpreters are actually getting their experience as interpreters in VRS settings. Julia, who has been an interpreter and interpreter educator for more than twenty years and holds a graduate degree in interpreting, complained about this situation:

Video relay centers are now hiring newbie [interpreters] who have never interpreted in the community to work in their centers. While [sign language interpreting trainers] have been working to emphasize the importance of knowing the context for several years, we are now seeing video relay service [providers] telling these newbie [interpreters] that the context is not important. They just want robots that will pick an English word for every sign. What a mess.

As Julia points out, there is a growing number of would-be interpreters who have not worked in the community and do not hold any certification but are now working in VRS centers. This is a point Peterson (forthcoming) makes poignantly clear when he talks about the skill necessary for producing effective interpretations when context is not provided. He states, "The success I have at the crucial guesswork of video interpreting is largely a function of my years of experience in the community and as an interpreter."

After years of attempting to produce literature and theory of sign language interpreting that calls for a complete understanding of the message before attempting to interpret, the field of interpreting now has to contend with moving backwards to a time when context is sacrificed for content. This is reminiscent of a model of interpreting long ago debunked (Weisenberg 2007; Stewart, Schein, and Cartwright 1998; Humphrey and Alcorn 1994). While this may provide for more expedient service to deaf and non-deaf callers, the reason these earlier models of interpreting, which did not emphasize complete understanding, were replaced was because they were found to be ineffective in producing the ultimate goal of communication between two people.

EMOTION WORK IN INTERPRETING

Just like deaf people, interpreters perform emotion work through the call. Although this work is sometimes a reaction to the behavior of a caller, it can also be seen as a by-product of remote interactions. This work is also part of working for a corporation.

Less-than-Courteous Callers

One manager told me that avoiding conversations with the deaf caller before the call begins prevents the interpreters from getting to know the deaf callers and potentially being biased for or against them. However, as we saw with Sarah and D. Vahded, biases can occur even when the interpreter does not have a conversation with the deaf caller before placing the call. Another example is provided by Tyler and his experience with someone he considered to be rude in the first few seconds of interaction:

The caller came up on my screen and I tried to do my introduction. You know, "Thank you for calling Ease Communication, Inc. VRS, I am interpreter number 4 . . ." She interrupted me. She said, "Same old thing. I don't need to know, just make the call." I told her that I would but that I had to give her my number. She didn't want it. I had to tell her that the FCC required me to tell her.

Tyler said he did not get upset by the caller's abrasiveness. He said, "The call wasn't going to continue until I gave her my number." He was able to control whether or not the caller received the information he felt he was obligated to provide. Tyler was also demonstrating who was in control of the call. Rebecca is another interpreter who exercised control over a call and attempted to teach courtesy to the deaf caller:

The caller came in and I saw where it was from. I said, "Hello. Thank you for using Ease Communication, Inc. How may I help you?" So I gave my introduction and the person just sat there. So I just sat there. He was busy doing some paperwork or something. He was writing on something. He looked up a few times and then he would start writing again. He then said, "Well?" I thought to myself, "You S.O.B. How dare you treat me like that?" I said, "How may I help you?" He got upset and said, "What the hell do you think I called in for? Just dial the number." I looked at him and said, "I said, How may I help you?" I made him say, "Please dial the number." I thought to myself, "Who do you think you are? You can't treat me like that."

While the actions of Tyler and Rebecca are about who controls the call, Theodore's comment demonstrates that interpreters also control perceptions:

When I know the person is going to be rude, I interpret more strictly to what I see. So I don't work to put it into English. Now, I don't think people have to thank me. I am getting paid. But when someone is just nice then I will work to make the message flow like a conversation.

From the stories provided by Theodore, Tyler, and Rebecca, it is not clear whether these deaf callers were in a bad mood, frustrated with the person they were attempting to call, or even frustrated with the interpreter's skill. What is clear is that callers deemed rude are reminded they have little power and in the case of Theodore, those callers who are judged to be "nice" will have their calls "flow more like a conversation."

Breuggemann (2004) witnessed the same type of events unfold at a conference she attended where there were interpreters who were "not quite qualified to interpret the level of international academic discourse" (68). The deaf people in attendance "began to ignore them, just sign-chatting among themselves and glancing occasionally at the real-time captioning screen" (68). The interpreters in this situation became "deadpan and their bodies registered their own mental, emotional absence from the scene and their job" (68).

Interpreters have different ways of dealing with behavior they construe as hostile. But in many of these situations, it appears that access is reserved for those deaf people who do not upset or offend the interpreter. Even though Theodore did not mention whether he implements the same punitive practice when he is in face-to-face interpreting assignments, the fact that he may not have to see this deaf caller again, because they do not share a community, may well influence his decision.

The experiences of Rebecca, Tyler, and Theodore underscore both that interpreters are human and that they can exercise power in the lives of deaf people. In a medium in which people do not have to interact with each other as complete people, in which they hear only a voice or see only a face and hands on a two-dimensional screen, it is easy for callers and interpreters to disregard each other as not human. These encounters demonstrate that at times interpreters can misuse the power they possess, as Theodore did. Finally, they demonstrate that interpreters have some investment in the callers, as shown in the responses of Tyler and Rebecca. Whether it is teaching them about phone etiquette, as Rebecca did, or reminding them of the governing bodies that organize the video relay industry, as Tyler did, the goal is to inform deaf people about how the call will proceed.

Investment in the Caller

Not every interpreter wants to be invested in the caller. In fact, some interpreters avoid getting "invested" altogether. Diane is one such interpreter who does not get invested in the lives of the people for whom she interprets on VRS. Her attitude in VRS situations is different than in face-to-face interpreting situations, as she explains:

On VRS I am not as invested. That is, I don't see that many people over and over again so I don't get to know them. When I worked in the educational arena, I took on more responsibilities in certain situations.

. . . So if I see the same person multiple times [while working in VRS] then I am more likely to invest myself. But I would say most of the time I never see the callers again.

Compassion for the well-being of your fellow citizen is often dependent on proximity. It is not altogether surprising that the lack of familiarity that VRS calls produce leads to a less invested interpreter. D. Vahded also suggests that in face-to-face interactions he is more invested in the outcome.

In part, my interest is selfish because regardless of what happens with that student's grades, it is going to come back and impact your life as the interpreter. If they pass, that means you did your job well enough for them to get the information they needed to move onto the next course. Of course, they also busted ass on their own. If they get an F it could be them, it could be the interpreter. I have been blamed many times for students failing.

Interpreters are often the easy target. The work of sign language interpreters is mostly discussed among practitioners. Although some academics who are not practitioners but consumers of interpreters' services have begun to take up the issue of interpreting as part of their analysis (e.g., Schwartz 2006; Brueggemann 2004; Padden and Humphries 2005), the work of interpreters is still largely misunderstood. When interpreters are involved, some people with little understanding of the significance of their role may not want to participate in (in)effective communication. After all, the interpreter is supposed to "make everything clear." Therefore, when a student fails a course or someone forgets an appointment, the interpreter is often considered to be at fault.

Customer Service: Representing the Goals of the Company

Up until this point, I have talked about interpreters representing their needs. However, in VRS, interpreters are representing the needs of the company they work for as well as their own needs. Sign language interpreters are the front-line employees of the VRS provider that employs them. Their primary responsibility is serving the customers. They are service professionals (Packham 1996), and their product or "commodity" (Marx [1867]1976, 127)—the interpretation—is being produced and consumed in real time. As part of this consumption, the interpreter is being evaluated. Given the nature of video relay interpreting and the venue in which it occurs, providers must rely on customer feedback to determine the quality of their product. Sign language interpreting is an interactive process. Through their body language, deaf people provide intepreters real-time feedback on the efficacy of an interpretation. Because the work of interpreting involves interaction between a service provider—the interpreter—and service recipients—deaf and non-deaf callers—this work can be considered what Leidner (1996) calls "interactive service work" (29). As such, deaf people and non-deaf people are as much a part of the process as the interpreter.

Estelle makes this point when she asks what is getting accounted for by Ease Communication:

> Do you want to be a company known for good customer service? Good customer service takes time. If I want to develop a rapport with this person, and the way I do it might be different than how someone else does it and it might be ok for me, and if you measure the amount of time it takes for us to develop this rapport and the amount of time it takes me is going to be different than the amount of time that it takes another person. Then what? If it doesn't meet your target, are you asking me to change the way I establish this rapport with them? Ok, then tell me how you want me to do that.

Some of the policies established by Ease Communication are designed to ensure that signed language interpreters will represent the company positively. There is a dress code. Interpreters are not to chew gum or eat while on the call; of course these are distracting behaviors, but with these policies Ease Communication is attempting to portray an image to the users of their service.

Margaret is clearer about what she does to positively represent Ease Communication. Margaret tells me about a call during which the deaf caller was holding a small child on her lap. The child was not sitting still and the caller had to hold onto her with one hand, which left only one hand free to communicate with the non-deaf caller through Margaret, and which made interpreting somewhat difficult for Margaret. At times, she was unable to understand everything the woman was saying. Rather than explaining to the deaf caller that it was difficult to understand her with only one hand, Margaret chose to say nothing. When I asked her why, she responded:

> I want this mother's experience with Ease Communication to be great. I didn't want her to become frustrated with the fact that her kid was

climbing all over her and that the interpreter may not understand her. I was getting what I could. But I didn't want her to get frustrated with my needs for both hands. I wanted her to have a good experience. I wanted her to use us again.

Even when the needs of the interpreter are counter to the comfort of the deaf caller, Margaret still suggests she does not impose upon the caller:

It is just like the people in the summertime that don't want to put their shirts on. I don't care. If they want to place a call without a shirt on then that is fine with me. I don't want to impose my needs on them. That is providing customer care and service. I am there with a smile saying, "That must suck but let's try the best we can."

Margaret understands that her employment is dependent on people continuing to use her service, which is perhaps more important now that the FCC requires videophones to be interoperable. If deaf people are unhappy with Ease Communication and the service they provide, Margaret, and many others, could be out of a job. However, Margaret also suggests that her behavior might have been different in a face-to-face situation:

It is a service industry and that is my idea of customer service. If she were frustrated and angry, then I could have gone there but she was calm. She seemed to be enjoying herself. She was just hanging out with her kid. If I were there in person, I could have perhaps given the kid my keys in my purse. I would've thought about what I had to keep the kid entertained. I would've taken more license [with it]. But I can't do that on the phone.

Other interpreters might have asked for a team or even transferred the call to another interpreter. Margaret seems to understand that her role is that of a representative for Ease Communication. She is not solely an interpreter. Her goal is greater than to provide access; it is to get repeat business as well. Fuller and Smith (1996) note that such judgments are a part of most interactive service work:

At one level management's definition of quality service is simple: quality service is being delivered when customers keep coming back and when they recommend a particular company to their friends. On the other hand exactly what prompts a customer to return and to recommend a company's service varies tremendously from individual to individual. As a consequence, interactive service workers are required to make on-the-spot, subtle judgments about what would please individual customers hundreds of thousands of times daily in the American workplace. (75)

Although a number of policies both from within Ease Communication and from the FCC are intended to create a standardized experience for users of this service, standardizing is problematic because of the human element. That is, as Leidner (1996) points out, two features of interactive service work make routinizing difficult. The first is the role of nonemployees—customers—in the interaction. It is difficult, if not impossible, to predict or control the actions of customers. Second, the item being sold is as much a product of the worker as it is of the corporation. Specifically in sign language interpreting, a great deal of personal choice goes into each interpretation. Interpreters must decide which signs to use and whether they are going to fingerspell a word or provide an initialized sign, among many other choices. Each of these choices is influenced by the interpreter's mood that day, his knowledge of the material, how many signs he know for a particular concept, and his assessment of the situation, to name a few contributing factors. It is because of these unknowns that the routinization of sign language interpreting is difficult.

CONCLUSION

When I first began my training, an instructor showed us a caricature of an interpreter standing up, with the aid of wires to enable standing indefinitely, and leg extensions, to give height if necessary. The interpreter has two extra arms and a band on one of them that will change the color of the shirt automatically to reduce eye strain. In one ear there is a surgically attached radar as to prevent the interpreter from missing the slightest sound, and on top of the interpreter's head is a computer so the interpreter can know everything instantly. To increase the insult, the interpreter's mouth is taped shut to prevent the revealing of any secrets, and the caricature includes a hydraulic boot that allows the deaf person to kick the interpreter in the rear when a mistake is made.

In addition to being funny, the illustration indicates the multiple demands of interpreting. It suggests the various factors that interpreters must take into consideration as they attempt to play cultural ambassador between two people. The drawing is dated, however; it would now be more accurate if it included a computer, perhaps strapped to the interpreter's back, a camera in the interpreter's face, and cables that not only assist in standing for long periods of time but also connect to "the politico-administrative regime" (G. Smith 1995, 21) that regulates signed language interpreters' behavior in VRS. The point is that interpreters do far more than just present one language in another. They also work in contexts that are sometimes known and sometimes unknown to them. The organization of VRS interpreting affords little opportunity to know the context of a call. Because VRS interpreting is a fairly new phenomenon, but likely here to stay, interpreters must begin to figure out how to teach the next generation of interpreters about the struggles they face in challenging situations and determine the multiple ways that video relay changes the work they perform.

Throughout this chapter, I have talked about the type of work that interpreters participate in that comes along with VRS interpreting, namely, the emotional, physical, and mental work they perform. The emotional and mental practices are invisible and cannot easily be accounted for on any form. Although they did not state this explicitly, interpreters did also suggest that they understand that their view of their job is different than the one they are held accountable for by Ease Communication. As I will discuss in chapter 5, the texts used to organize the practice of VRS take into account only visible practices that can be recorded. Using these narratives, we can see what these interpreters consider to be important aspects of their work. Next we will turn to that which is considered important in the context of ruling relations, and thus is documented to make interpreters accountable.

Chapter 5

Textualizing the "On Call"

and "Off Call" Interpreter

Before 1990, access in the public sphere for people with disabilities was a luxury that depended on the kindness of others. The passage of the ADA made access for people with disabilities a right. Once the goal was established, states had to create a mechanism by which they could guarantee this goal, and create a protocol for measuring how well they achieved it.

As a service that is provided by the federal government to promote the right of access outlined in the ADA, VRS is connected to a complex of practices that coordinate its delivery and reception. In this time of privatization, the government has subcontracted the provision of telephone access for deaf people to for-profit organizations, such as Ease Communication, and therefore must consider issues of employment, payment, management, efficiency, and profit. As individuals who engage VRS as service receivers or service providers, deaf people and sign language interpreters and the work they perform vis-à-vis VRS becomes a product of this coordination. This coordination is necessitated by and connected to definitions of disability, the ADA, and the FCC.

This coordination, in the form of policies, occurs over great distances and is possible through the use of various texts that are taken up and acted upon by interpreters, schedulers, managers, and regulatory agencies. It extends to users of VRS as policies are conveyed to deaf and non-deaf callers through the direct and indirect behaviors of interpreters. Frequent users of VRS begin to incorporate these policies into their everyday use of the service.

There are multiple aspects of VRS that could be measured, such as the amount of work, visible and invisible, done by deaf people who use the service, and whether deaf callers are satisfied with the service and, if not, which aspects of the service would they like to be improved upon. Deaf and non-deaf callers and interpreters could be surveyed about the effectiveness of a given call, which could also yield useful information. The texts used in VRS indicate and capture other important aspects of VRS: the amount of time it takes an interpreter to connect to both callers and the number of minutes per hour an interpreter is connected to both callers. In this chapter, I discuss these texts and their role in organizing interpreters' work in VRS.

I must begin where we will eventually end, with "functionally equivalent," the language that appears in Title IV of the ADA. Two questions are pertinent to the discussion that follows: (a) What is "functionally equivalent"? and (b) How is it determined? In the case of video relay service, "functionally equivalent" is measured by the FCC to gauge how much VRS resembles the telephone service of non-deaf people. What do those services look like?

It is helpful here to provide a laundry list much like the one Peggy McIntosh (1988) provided in "White Privilege: The Invisible Knapsack." Granted, this list will not be as extensive as McIntosh's; my point is merely to provide the context for the discussion that follows rather than enumerate the many privileges I share with other non-deaf people who function in a society that favors the ability to hear.

As a non-deaf person, I can pick up a phone and call whomever I would like, if I have their number. I am able to place calls at any hour of the day. In addition, I can feel confident that when I am traveling on the road, in the city, if my car were to break down, I could find a phone that I could use to place a call to a tow truck or friend to help me. In my home, I can, for an additional fee, call friends through three-way calling, or through call-waiting have a call interrupted by another person. And perhaps most functional in my use of the phone is my ability to place the receiver on my shoulder and walk around the house cleaning and cooking, if I were so inclined. I am also able to go out and sit on the front porch and talk to friends and family while watching my neighbor, who is sitting on her porch talking to friends and family. Finally, for most of my calls, I share a language with the person to whom I am speaking and do not have to rely on a third person to mediate my call; therefore, I am fairly certain that the message I send will be received by the intended party and that my business, be it personal or professional, will be addressed.

Functionally speaking, the telephone has made my life more convenient in that I can converse with people in various places in the world. Since phones, and their subsequent features, were designed for and by non-deaf people, it makes sense that I, a non-deaf person, benefit. What about people who are deaf? In what ways can a phone service for deaf and hard of hearing people be comparable to the service of non-deaf people? These questions were part of the thinking, or so it seems, that led to the development of the traditional relay service and later VRS.

Some of the aspects of non-deaf telephone service are not accessible to deaf telephone users. For example, it is unreasonable to expect that a deaf person would need or want to place any type of phone on her shoulder as she walks around the room. She simply would not be able to see the person she was talking to. However, it is not unrealistic to expect that a deaf caller would be able to convey her message to the intended party and that her business would be addressed.

As with all services regulated by the federal government, these services have to be managed and measured. Furthermore, relay services, regardless of modality, have to be deemed functionally equivalent to those telephone services that non-deaf persons receive. To understand how these three requirements are met, we must examine various texts and their role in organizing this service.

THE ROLE OF TEXTS IN ORGANIZING PRACTICES

People's activities are tied to complexes—institutions—that are located in multiple sites and are multilayered. I draw my conceptualization of institutions from Dorothy Smith (2006), who describes an institution as various practices that are coordinated around a single focus (D. Smith 2005), and not a physical location, per se. As such, there must be mechanisms by which people in various sites and with various functions can be synchronized. Through the use of texts, as we saw with how a qualified interpreter is defined, people can perform this coordination. As Dorothy Smith (2005) reminds us, "Institutions exist in that strange magical realm in which social relations based on texts transform the local particularities of people, place, and time into standardized, generalized, and, especially translocal forms of coordinating people's activities" (101).

Texts can be in different forms. "They have in common, however, this one effect, that they are forms of writing, speaking, or imaging that are replicable and hence can be read, heard, and watched by more than one individual, in different places, and at different times" (D. Smith 2005, 165). Texts are used as a means of ruling and institutional ethnography is designed to reveal the ways in which texts are used in the organization of everyday activities (DeVault 2006). Although an examination of the texts and how they are activated is important to understand the organization of the provision of VRS, they are not the foci; I examine, and understand them, as an impetus for actions that join various practices.

> The text is analyzed for its characteristically textual form of participation in social relations. The interest is in the social organization of those relations and in penetrating them, discovering them, opening them up from within, through the text. The texts enters the laboratory, so to speak, carrying the threads and shreds of the relations it is organized by and organizes. The text before the analyst, then, is not used as a specimen or sample, but as a means of access, a direct line to the relations it organizes. (D. Smith 1990a, 4)

Texts are often used for accounting purposes. "Accounting, rather than being a simple matter of neutral record-keeping after the fact, plays an active conceptual role in setting the terms in which organizational activities can be thought, discussed and evaluated" (McCoy 1998, 396). These texts appear in the form of rules or legislative mandates, reports, and standards, to name a few. The goal is not to examine the form these texts take but to explore "the intersection of the extended social relations of ruling through an actual experience of reading. Hence analysis focuses on just that intersection, on how the reader operates the text to just enter the objectified modes of knowing characteristics of the relations of ruling" (D. Smith 1990a, 5). In doing so, we see how personalized and diverse, and sometimes messy, actions, such as sign language interpreting, get reduced into a sterile "one size fits all" category that can be counted, cataloged, and understood in an objectified form.

As I began this project, I struggled to understand how and when texts were activated and by whom. The practice of sign language interpreting is, for the most part, undocumented, or so I thought. Texts do appear in the field of sign language interpreting. In fact, our credentials, work history or vitae, and applications for jobs (e.g., videotapes) are all forms of texts that move among interpreters and are used to document our work. However, texts, as tangible objects, are passed from one interpreter to the next in the field of interpreting far less frequently than they are in medical work, for example, as cases are charted in order to coordinate the work of a health-care team. Nevertheless, I soon discovered that texts are being activated in VRS. Therefore, part of my goal was to seek out when and how this occurs.

Aside from the actual texts that are used by interpreters, the presence of texts becomes apparent through the discourses used by interpreters, managers, and schedulers. These texts via discourses appear in policies that are relayed to interpreters-in-training. Their verbiage (and idioms) becomes part of the vernacular of practitioners as we talk about what it is we do.

The texts I focus on here were produced at different times and in different locations, but they were designed and deployed so as to come together to document and organize the work of sign language interpreters. Here, I am interested in the ways in which various texts, as extensions of ruling relations, organize the work of interpreters in VRS by operationalizing the policies and mandates of Ease Communication and the government. Ruling relations is a concept that institutional ethnographers use to talk about the web of practices that encompasses "power, organization, direction, and regulation" (D. Smith 1987, 3). It is "that total complex of activities, differentiated into many spheres, by which our kind of society is ruled, managed, and administered. It includes what the business world calls *management*, it includes the professions, it includes government and the activities of those who are selecting, training, and indoctrinating those who will be its governors" (D. Smith 1990b, 14) and serves as the focus for investigation (D. Smith 1999). To explore this process I look behind the phrase "functional equivalence" in an attempt to unmask peoples' actual doings. This is an attempt to make those practices "accessible" (Eastwood 2006).

THE AMERICANS WITH DISABILITIES ACT AND THE FCC: CONNECTING THE ACT WITH THE SERVICE

The Standard Practice Paper on Video Interpreting produced by RID states:

> Never before, in the history of the interpreting profession, have interpreters worked in settings where the federal government and large corporations have played such an important role in the provision of interpreting services.

This proclamation points to two issues: first, that the oversight of the work of interpreters is increased within this particular setting; and second, that this remote supervision requires an increase in the textual practices that can standardize conduct. These texts can be actual texts that are taken up and filled out or texts that are merely referred to. Regardless of the way in which the texts are presented, they serve as a means of justifying, organizing, and documenting work. Furthermore, these texts are often left vague, which gives the application some flexibility (Carey 2009).

"Functionally equivalent" is a term used in Title IV of the ADA, which describes the relay services for the deaf and states that services for people with disabilities must be functionally equivalent to those of people without disabilities. The ADA does not provide a definition of this seemingly significant phrase, however. Instead it only states:

> The term "telecommunications relay services" means telephone transmission services that provide the ability for an individual who has a hearing impairment or speech impairment to engage in communication by wire or radio with a hearing individual in a manner that is *functionally equivalent* to the ability of an individual who does not have a hearing impairment or speech impairment to communicate using voice communication services by wire or radio. Such term includes services that enable two-way communication between an individual who uses a TDD or other nonvoice terminal device and an individual who does not use such a device. (47 U.S.C. § 225 (a)(3))

The ADA provides the terminology, but the means by which functional equivalency is measured is left to the FCC. The FCC has enacted various rules to achieve this end.

In 2000, the FCC expanded the definition of telecommunication relay service to include VRS. The following is in the introductory paragraph of the notice from the FCC released on March 6, 2000:

> With this Order, we amend the rules governing the delivery of telecommunications relay services to expand the kinds of relay services available to consumers and to improve the quality of relay services, based on our ten years of experience with Telecommunications Relay Service (TRS) and changes in available technologies. Title IV of the Americans with Disabilities Act of 1990 (ADA), which is codified at section 225 of the Communications Act of 1934, as amended ("Communications Act"), requires the Commission to ensure that TRS is available, to the extent possible and in the most efficient manner, to individuals with hearing and speech disabilities in the United States.[21] Section 225 de-

---

21. Pub. L. No. 101-336, § 401, 104 Stat. 327, 366-69 (1990) (adding section 225 to the Communications Act of 1934, as amended, 47 U.S.C. § 225).

fines relay service to be a telephone transmission service that provides the ability for an individual with a hearing or speech disability to engage in communication by wire or radio with a hearing individual in a manner *functionally equivalent* to someone without such a disability.[22] Section 225 requires the Commission to ensure that interstate and intrastate relay services are available throughout the country and to establish regulations to ensure the quality of relay service.[23] To fulfill this mandate, the Commission first issued rules in 1991.[24] TRS has been available on a uniform, nationwide basis since July 26, 1993.[25]

Within this paragraph, the FCC connects the goal of functional equivalency with the ADA. Functional equivalency is the clearly stated goal, but the phrase is left undefined.

FCC requirements for VRS include that 80 percent of all calls be answered in less than two minutes and that the interpreter, the deaf caller, and the non-deaf caller all must be in different locations. If the deaf and non-deaf callers are in the same location, the service is no longer called VRS, but instead it is considered video remote interpreting, which is not currently under the jurisdiction of the FCC. In 2006, the FCC established another mandate, which was that VRSs had to be made available twenty-four hours a day.

VRS is funded by a phone tax. In the United States, there are a number of VRS providers; all of them are for-profit organizations. As with any business, mergers and acquisitions make it difficult to identify the exact number of providers. Many of the companies provided a videophone free to deaf people and until 2006 required them to place calls only through their service. I had heard Ease Communication representatives compare

22. 47 U.S.C. § 225(a)(3).

23. Ibid., at § 225(b).

24. 47 C.F.R. § 64.604; Telecommunications Services for Individuals with Hearing and Speech Disabilities, and the Americans with Disabilities Act of 1990, CC Docket No. 90-571, Report and Order and Request for Comments, 6 FCC Rcd 4657 (1991) (*First Report and Order*).

25. Under section 225, common carriers providing telephone voice transmission services were required to begin providing TRS, throughout the areas they served, as of July 26, 1993. *See* 47 U.S.C. § 225(c). Prior to this time, some states offered relay services, but the services offered differed from state to state, and were subject to many limitations. *See* Strauss, Title IV - Telecommunications, in *Implementing the Americans with Disabilities Act* at 156–158 (Gostin & Beyer 1993).

this practice to that of cellular phone service providers. The argument, as they stated it, was that people who get a phone from Verizon, for example, are not able to place calls through T-Mobile; therefore, why should people be allowed to use Ease Communication equipment to call through one of its competitors? The FCC ostensibly disagreed with this analogy because in 2006, the FCC released its VRS interoperability announcement:

> In response to a petition by the California Coalition of Agencies Serving the deaf and Hard of Hearing, the FCC has found that all VRS consumers must be able to place a VRS call through any VRS provider's service, and all VRS providers must be able to receive calls from, and make calls to, any VRS consumer. The Commission also determined that restricting the use of a provider's VRS service so that consumers cannot access other VRS providers is inconsistent with the functional equivalency mandate, the public interest and the intent of Congress. (http://www.fcc.gov/cgb/dro/trs_history_docket.html)

After this announcement, regardless of which provider installed the videophone, a caller could use any VRS provider he chose. This meant that users could go where, in their judgment, the best interpreters were working. Whereas some deaf people did choose which VRS provider they would use based on the interpreters, most deaf people I spoke with said that their choice of provider was a matter of convenience: they chose the service that had the shortest wait time.

This increased competition created by the FCC's ruling inspired VRS providers to be more vigilant in improving their services for deaf callers. Ease Communication saw standardization as a means by which they could improve their services; hence, training for signed language interpreters was needed.

CREATING STANDARDIZATION

Smith (1990a) suggests institutional ethnographers start with the everyday; therefore, I begin with a training I attended for Ease Communication in 2007. There were eight sign language interpreters in the training room and we were in teleconference with another site that had approximately ten interpreters. All of the people in the training were people who provided interpreting in VRS; each had various years of experience in the field of interpreting.

During the training, the trainer discussed the goal of a standardized product. It was clear that the trainer saw our work—the interpretation—as a product that is purchased on a per-minute basis by the FCC. Those of us in attendance were trying to convey the complexity of our work and suggest that our interpretation could be ineffective if it were standardized because people, who are integral to our work, are not standard.

The trainer explained that "it is important to have standardization in our process." I immediately began to question the feasibility of "standardizing" interpreting. Is it possible? Unlike in mathematics or chemistry, no easy formula consistently yields a successful interpretation. There are too many unknowns that must be taken into consideration, questions such as the following: What is the language preference of the deaf caller? What is the context of the interaction (e.g., why are these people talking to each other)? What are the limitations the interpreter, based on skill and comfort with subject matter, brings to the interaction? How comfortable is the nonsigning, non-deaf person with the process of VRS? What are the moods of all the people involved: interpreter, deaf caller, and non-deaf caller? As Smith (2006) aptly points out, "People, as individuals, arrive at any moment with their own distinctive histories, their distinctive perspectives, capacities, interests, concerns, and whatever else they may bring as a potentiality to act in a given setting" (65). All of these variables will impact the call. I am sure the trainer, a sign language interpreter herself, recognized that these variables (and many others) exist and thus make it difficult to "standardize" interpreting. Yet, here she was telling us we need to "standardize our processes." It was quite the conundrum.

The processes the trainer was instructing us to standardize ranged from the information we could share with the caller to what we could allow the caller to see us doing. We all knew we were unable to share our names and which city we were in with either caller. We also knew that we should be "off camera" if we were going to get a drink, fix our clothes or headsets, or do anything else that required us to not focus on the caller. Each of us had, in our own ways, come to grips with these rules. Now, however, we were also told how and what to interpret.

When a deaf caller places a call, the interpreter is supposed to interpret the information he hears on the phone, but we were being asked to place limits on the information we passed on to callers. For example, there is a noticeable difference between a busy signal that indicates someone is on the line versus a busy signal that indicates two or more calls are dropping into the phone line at the same time. The former is a slow busy signal while the latter is a faster busy signal. The second type of busy signal can also mean that the phone line is down. During this meeting we were instructed that we could not tell callers whether the signal was fast or slow. Instead, we were instructed to "tell them that the line is busy (signing BUSY) and ask them if they wish to make another call."

In addition to telling us how and what to convey to the deaf person, we were also told that we could "no longer tell the hearing person whether the phone is ringing, busy, or turned off" (all information we can see when we dial the number). Most of the people in training did not mind not telling the non-deaf people that the phone was turned off but drew the line when it came to not telling the non-deaf person that the phone was busy or ringing.

The reason for the unrest was stated by an interpreter who said, "That just seems unfair. We work for both the deaf person and the hearing person." As she continued, she explained that whether the phone is ringing or busy is information that belongs to the callers, not the interpreter. And if we did not interpret it by telling the non-deaf person what we saw, we would not be conveying the message accurately. The trainer, apparently unconvinced, simply stated, "We all need to be doing the same thing."

As I glanced around the room, I noticed people with perplexed looks on their faces. However, with the exception of one or two other people, nobody shared their concerns with the goal of "standardizing" our work. A few people began to raise their hands and state all of the reasons that standardization and interpreting were incompatible. When people began to suggest different scenarios when a particular practice may not work, the trainer immediately shut down that discussion by reiterating the importance of standardization. I was not convinced of the importance of standardization.

In the managerial view, standardizing our work is a means to an end, not the end in itself. The reason for standardizing is simple. This form of Fordism increases the probability of interchangeability (Ritzer 1996). When practices are standard, organizations are able to move people around without regard to differences in skill. In VRS this means using a computer program to assign hours to interpreters, rather than depend on managers or schedulers who understand the work involved to evaluate each interpreter and determine when and where each is needed. In addition, because of the unpredictability of VRS calls—the content can range from legal matters to ordering a pizza—it behooves corporations to have a standard practice so they do not have to rely on the discretion and experience of individual interpreters. Standardizing practices also allow companies to hire interpreters with little or no experience. Employees become seen as a resource to be allocated rather than people with professional skills.

To achieve functional equivalency, VRS is systematized and monitored. Standardization of the work of interpreters is one aspect of this process. Standardization allows corporations, such as Ease Communication, to identify the desired practices that will lead to functional equivalency. Once management has decided which activities indicate a functionally equivalent service, they can then work to make those activities visible and can begin an accounting of those activities (McCoy 1998).

MAKING SIGNED LANGUAGE INTERPRETING WORK VISIBLE

A great deal of the work of sign language interpreters is invisible. An interpreted message is the product of extensive mental processing (Cokely 1988). Interpreters take a message presented in its original form, ASL or English, and analyze the message for purpose and meaning. Once the interpreter feels he understands the meaning behind the message, he begins to reconstruct the message using the grammatically correct features of the target form, ASL or English. Other than seeing the work of waiting, listening, and the actual interpretation, onlookers are unable to witness this process. Arguably, the most difficult part of the work is never seen.

Another way to think about the work of sign language interpreters is to imagine that people come to a given interaction with ideas and plans for the interaction and the job of an interpreter is to take those ideas and convey them to another person who uses a different language. "People who speak different languages and come from differing cultural backgrounds experience the world in different manners; they have different *thought worlds*" (Dean and Pollard 2005, 261). One way to think about a "thought world" is to imagine the following scenario:

> I grew up in Phoenix, Arizona. It is called the Valley of the Sun. It is so named because it is surrounded on all sides by mountains. About eight years ago, a group of friends and I all decided to rent a car and take a road trip to California. While there, we drove to Beverly Hills and decided to admire the beautiful homes. We drove slowly as we talked about the ornate, larger than life, homes. We did not realize that behind us was a car filled with young women who were not interested

in sight seeing but wanted to get to their destination. They honked at us, getting our attention, and we quickly pulled over to the side of the road to allow them to pass. As they passed us, the driver yelled out the window, "Why don't you go back to the Valley!" At first, we were shocked that they knew we were from the Valley of the Sun. We soon realized that they were insulting us by implying we were from "the Valley," an area in Southern California, and the implication was that we were obviously not from Beverly Hills.

Another example is the word "fag" and its use in Europe and in the United States. In Europe, "fag" can refer to a cigarette, whereas in the United States, it is a derogatory term for a gay man. A person from Europe visiting the United States might raise some eyebrows if he were to ask where to buy some fags.

These examples demonstrate the way in which thought worlds are important to effective communication. The thought world of the speaker in the narrative was situated in Arizona, where "the Valley" had a specific meaning. That meaning was not shared by the women in the other car in Beverly Hills. The work of interpreters is to understand one person's thought world and interpret it to another person. Ingram (cited in Stewart, Schein, and Cartwright 1998, 45–46) explains this process:

> A message is first coded for transmission—a process called *encoding*. The code may be English, ASL, or nonlanguages such as gestures, facial expressions, or grunts. The message is then transmitted over a *channel* (e.g., speech or writing). When received, it is *decoded* (i.e., put into a form accessible to the receiver). Any signal that interferes with transmission of the message is labeled *noise*.

This process is further complicated when an interpreter is inserted. That is, after the message is coded for transmission by the sender, the ASL interpreter must decode the message from its original language (e.g., visual or spoken) and then encode the message in the target language and begin transmission. At that time, the receiver of the message begins their own coding and decoding process.

Sign language interpreters, with very few exceptions, traditionally have worked autonomously. The interpreter is often the only person in a given setting who is able to understand both languages being used and is left to their own scruples to determine the correct course of action in each situation. This could include reinterpreting to clarify, requesting time to assess the effectiveness of a given interpretation, or even stopping the interaction to inform one or both parties that an error in interpretation has been made. Along with those issues that are directly related to the interpretation, in face-to-face interpreting, interpreters are solely responsible of taking care of themselves. This means they rely on their own judgment to determine when a break is needed and to negotiate with the clients how to proceed. Although the industry standards for face-to-face interpreting suggest that interpreters should not work more than one and half hours alone, some interpreters, for a variety of reasons, may choose to work a little longer or a little less than the standard.

The increased employment opportunities for sign language interpreters offered by the development of VRSs have been accompanied by new forms of management within new commercial enterprises. The managers in these new organizations need ways to make interpreters accountable. Therefore, they must make certain aspects of interpreters' work visible and thereby countable. Various texts have been created to achieve this goal.

TEXTS AND THEIR ROLES IN EASE COMMUNICATION AND BEYOND

In order to make the work of interpreters visible and measurable to management and to other interpreters, Ease Communication employs various texts. Some of the texts are produced inside the call center and move beyond the center to other entities in order to account for the work of interpreters. Other texts are produced outside of the center and used in the center to demonstrate accountability. In addition to making the work of interpreters visible, some texts, such as the Kudos Certificate, are a visible representation of the work of deaf and non-deaf users of VRS, as these texts are used to document feedback to Ease Communication.

Whereas the design and layout of each text organizes its use, the role of the users of these texts is also significant. That is, texts also draw the reader's attention to what is considered significant by those who take up these texts. The Kudos Certificate provides insight to the recipient of the certificate and to Ease Communication on what deaf and non-deaf callers consider worth mentioning about the services they received. Other texts, such as those which calculate time of interpreting, demonstrate the significance of call processing and efficiency as understood by interpreters, Ease Communication, and the FCC.

Kudos as Accountability

All texts are the product of someone's work. Institutional texts are typically created in an attempt to organize those who come in contact with them. Even the most benevolent institutional text has a motive to organize behavior. Therefore, directionality is an important component to understanding the role of texts. Some texts, perhaps even most, originate as part of the employee's work but move into the administrative realm and are taken up as part of the administrative team's work. These texts are those that the employee activates first and include time cards and activity reports. Other texts are made in another location and sent to the place where the employee and management team will be able to activate them. That is, they are able to take up the text and use it to further a particular goal.

One such text that is produced in the administrative realm and sent to the employee's workplace is a text that demonstrates appreciation. I have called it a "Kudos Certificate." Figure 5.1 represents one of these Kudos Certificates.

Kudos Certificates adorned the wall of one center I worked in. In the other center, there were similar certificates but far fewer. These certificates are conspicuously posted so that every person who enters the center is able to see who received a compliment from a caller.

Kudos Certificates are the result of a caller (typically a deaf caller but non-deaf callers can also initiate the process) who calls or sends an email to the customer service department at the corporate offices of Ease Communication and compliments a particular interpreter by her or his number. At the bottom of the certificate, in the deaf caller's English, is the caller's complimentary statement.

Some interpreters have multiple certificates on the wall while others have none. D. Vahded indicates his frustration because the certificate does not mean anything in terms of increasing his hours or pay:

FIGURE 5.1. *Kudos Certificate.*

If someone is like, "Oh this interpreter is awesome," then you would think that they would be paid more. It doesn't happen. How many people have those Certificates of Excellence? I don't know how many . . . you know those people who say, "You are an awesome interpreter. You are the best! I want you every time." All you get for that is a piece a paper on the wall."

What purpose, if any, do these Kudos Certificates have? Like D. Vahded says, they do not increase the likelihood that an interpreter will get extra hours or pay. What they do is much more subtle. They represent the ideal to other interpreters. Much like the Rolls Royce represents the hard work of the woman who drives it or the Rolex represents smart investments, the Kudos Certificates are used by management to show interpreters that they too could have their name on the wall. However, just like the Rolls Royce and the Rolex, the Kudos Certificate does not represent an accurate picture of the work or luck required to get such a symbol.

One interpreter told me that when a deaf person complimented him during a call he was interpreting, he would immediately give the deaf person the number and email and tell her to contact the customer service department so he could get a certificate. Lewis, who at last count had over seven certificates, said:

I don't take them seriously. I think they are really fucking stupid. But for some reason [the manager] likes to place them on the wall. Right now, there are a few of us who are just trying to get as many callers [as we can] to call in and give us a compliment. We really don't take them seriously though.

Since Ease Communication is not permitted, currently, to record calls made through VRS, there is no practical way for them to directly assess the quality of the service they are providing. Although D. Vahded and Lewis suggest that the Kudos Certificates are treated by interpreters as something of a joke, in some ways the certificates are intended to operate as an indirect quality control measure, through what Fuller and Smith (1996) call "customer control" or "management by customers" (78). Kudos Certificates achieve this goal, even if they are viewed as a joke. Using the Kudos Certificate to encourage interpreters to provide quality service is one way to achieve a productive worker. Another alternative could involve a more direct practice, such as call monitoring. However, van den Broek (2004) points out that because "management of interactive service workers relies on the need to elicit tacit skills, which deliver quality output as well as specified quantities of output, it is also not surprising that coercive and direct control may often be counterproductive" (4).

Like Kudos Certificates, complaints are initiated by the deaf or non-deaf caller through the customer service department. These too provide a textual trail. However, they are not, for confidentiality reasons, posted on the walls.

Time Cards

The Kudos Certificates represent one type of text, initiated by customers and used internally. Other types of texts are initiated within Ease Communication and are rarely, if ever, seen by users of VRS. One such text is the time card, which is used by interpreters to document their time. The time card is a complex Excel spreadsheet that can be filled out at each station or at home by the interpreters. The form can then be emailed or printed out and placed in the mailbox of the manager of the center.

Time cards, as a means to stand in for the actual worker, contain a lot of identifying information about the interpreter: the center he worked in during the pay period being billed for, his hourly rate, and his mailing address and employee number. Interpreters also document the dates, times, and shifts they work.

The time of shift will impact whether the interpreter receives a differential, 10 percent more than the regular hourly rate for night shifts and weekend shifts, and 20 percent more than the hourly rate for graveyard hours. (The night shift starts at 7:00 P.M. and the graveyard shift starts at 12:00 A.M. and ends at 6:00 A.M.) After the interpreter inputs the rate and the number of hours in the correct columns (Day Hours, Nights/Weekend Hours, Graveyard or Holiday), the formulas in the spreadsheet calculate the pay for the interpreter.

Interpreter Efficiency: Calculating "On Call" vs. "Off Call"

By far the majority of texts used in VRS are those that are produced inside the center and used by the "home office" to produce more texts and demonstrate accountability to governmental, funding, and other coordinating organizations. Amber explained to me that there are two states of being for interpreters: "on call" and "off call." This does not mean actually interpreting a call but refers to the availability of an interpreter. When an interpreter is in his station, available to take a call, he is considered to be "on call" or available for a call. Interpreters are considered "off call," when they are unavailable to accept a call because they are working on a project or away from their stations.

To account for an interpreter's productivity, there are three different reports produced within the center's computer system. These reports are the Log, the Productivity Report, and the Minutes Generated Report. Jacob, a manager, mentioned another report, saying, "There is surely another report that tracks interpreter's speed of answer, but I haven't seen it." Jacob suggests it is this report, which he has not seen, that allows Ease Communication and other VRS providers to measure their compliance with the speed of answer set by the FCC, which states that 80 percent of all calls during a month must be answered within 120 seconds.

Activity Log

The Activity Log is used by interpreters to document when they are "off call" or otherwise not available to produce billable minutes and thus are not generating money for Ease Communication. The Log is submitted weekly. Interpreting does not have to be occurring for an interpreter to be producing minutes; as long as both callers are connected, the interpreter is producing minutes to be reimbursed by the FCC. In certain situations, such as when a deaf caller has placed a call to a paging company like T-Mobile and she is placed on hold for extended periods of time while the T-Mobile representative investigates the problem being reported, there may be no interpreting occurring even though both people are connected.

The Log does not account for every possible situation. Instead, interpreters are able to use it for the most common occurrences. When filling out the Log, interpreters must note the start and end times that they are off call or not producing minutes, for example, when they are sitting at their station talking with a colleague about a particular call (i.e., receiving mentoring). Then they must total their minutes. The categories commonly used for interpreters not producing minutes are Technical, Handoff, Team, Training, and Other.

An interpreter can indicate technical reasons for not producing minutes when there is a problem with the system. Occasionally, an interpreter gets locked out of the system because of a computer glitch. To solve this issue, he sends a message to the technical department and asks to be "killed in the system." The technical staff kicks the interpreter out of the system so that he can then log back in.

When a call is beyond the skill of an interpreter, begins to cut into the interpreter's lunch, or break, or requires the interpreter to stay beyond her shift, she can hand the call off to another interpreter. Using the handoff option is different than placing the call back in queue. When a call is placed back in the queue, any interpreter within Ease Communication who is logged on can receive the call. A "handoff" is when the call is taken over by another interpreter within the same center. Furthermore, it requires an interpreter to log off her or his station and take over the call at another station. Because this time is tallied as producing minutes for the original interpreter who handed the call off to another interpreter, the second interpreter must document that she was on a handoff call, accounting for the portion of her shift that is not documented in the system.

Teaming is similar to the handoff category. When an interpreter seeks assistance from another interpreter for a call, there is no record of the second interpreter for the time they are working with the other interpreter. This usually includes providing support in terms of helping the initial interpreter understand a heavy accent of a non-deaf person or understanding the signs of the deaf person. It can also include preventing the initial interpreter from becoming exhausted if the call happens to continue for several hours.

"Training" indicates that an interpreter is not producing minutes because she is with management. Because policies, regulations, and the computer equipment change frequently, there are times when management must sit with interpreters to explain a new procedure.

All other incidents that are not covered by these categories can be placed in the "Other" category. I used this category when I was locked out of the center because I forgot my key, for example, and when I interpreted a meeting between my manager and his colleagues.

The goal is to account for any time the interpreter is not "on call" so that the interpreter's efficiency can be calculated more accurately. However, the Log is used not only to hold interpreters responsible. Management can use the Log also to see how often technical issues prevent interpreters from producing minutes. They can see how long training is taking. Even though the interpreters fill out the forms, the forms are also used to monitor the work of others in the organization.

These reports, although beneficial for Ease Communication, change how interpreters perform their work. Estelle, who in the previous chapter compared our work to that of an ambassador, said:

> One of the biggest things is this concept of our work being evaluated in numeric form, which is not . . . which you don't experience in the

community. So things like, for example, how long you are on a call. How efficiently you end one call and pick up another call. It is sort of how they measure these little bits of a task, which is corporate because they want to see how a particular process is flowing. Is the process breaking down? And how can we make it more efficient so we can get more "bang for our buck"? I totally get that. Having that scheme imposed on us as interpreters . . . it's a different way of thinking about the work that we do.

Estelle's use of the term "efficient" indicates that she has begun to adopt the discourse of Ease Communication. She recognizes that "efficient" implies a streamlining of processes. She knows that the goal of Ease Communication is to produce an environment, and employee, in which every movement is money-producing so that the company "gets more bang for their buck." To move toward this efficient practice, Ease Communication requires interpreters to fill out the Log.

One important point is that the Log makes interpreters accountable to the organization, rather than to the users. The Log does not provide any space for a discussion or documentation of the practice of interpreting itself (e.g., the actual interpretation). Instead, numerical data is used simply to determine when interpreters are not processing calls. Measurable outcomes are seen in terms of minutes spent interpreting on the phone and not whether that time resulted in effective interpretations. This allows management to analyze and determine where changes can be made, if possible, to ensure that interpreters are on the phone more.

Many of the interpreters did not know what happened to the report after they filled it out and placed it in the scheduler's mailbox. One interpreter, Diane, told me, "It just helps them know when we are off the phones. I am not sure how helpful it is though. When I remember, I just check a box. I never really think about why I am off the phone, I just want to make note that I was off the phone." Another one said, "I guess it could be used to pay us." The reality is that the Log is used as an internal management tool, to explain the breaks in time on the Productivity Report.

PRODUCTIVITY REPORT

Whereas the Log is used within the particular VRS centers, the Productivity Report (see figure 5.2) moves outside the center; it is sent to the corporate office and used there to tally minutes to bill the FCC. Once the interpreter submits a timecard, the manager compares it to the Productivity Report and Log. This is how Ease Communication ensures that the interpreters are working during the time they are being paid. "Each month," Amber explains, "we must submit the total number of minutes each interpreter was 'on call' and 'off call' to headquarters." As Amber explained her process for submitting these numbers for her interpreters, she also tells me about how she uses the information contained in the reports:

> These [two reports] are used within the centers. I use them to see if my people are doing what they are supposed to be doing. They aren't given to the FCC. Once I have adjusted an interpreter's Productivity Report, I submit both documents to headquarters and they archive them . . . I think. I want to see how many times my interpreters are off the phones without a reason. I am bit of a hard ass. I don't mind if people want to take breaks but if they are taking too many breaks then that will affect their coworkers and I can't have that happening. So I use the information to help me manage my interpreters.

The term "adjusted" here seems to indicate a practice of managerial oversight within the corporation. The data I collected do not allow for a detailed examination of how this adjustment is accomplished, or how adjusted figures are used, at the managerial level. It is clear, however, that these forms ask interpreters to account closely for their time, and especially for any time when they are not producing minutes that are billable.

Each Productivity Report documents the time an interpreter has logged in and logged out of the phone system. This report does not inform the reader whether the interpreter whose activity is documented here is actually interpreting. The log-in times help management know when the interpreter became available to accept calls. This is not the time that is billed to the FCC. This time is important when calculating "setup" time, or the time required to get ready to accept calls. Furthermore, it shows management whether the interpreter arrived on time for her or his shift and when an interpreter is unavailable for calls. In the report recreated in figure 5.2, we see that the first line of the report shows the interpreter logged in and was "on call" at 10:04 A.M. Assuming the interpreter's start time was 10:00 A.M., there would be a corresponding entry on the Log that would start at 10:00 A.M. and end at 10:04 A.M. and provide an explanation for the four minutes. If the time is not explained on the Log then it will appear to be "setup" time. Furthermore, if we look at the sixth and seventh lines of logging in and out times for 06/07/2009, we

Interpreting Center	Username	Last	First	Date	Login Time		Logout Time		Minutes
	Interpreter	Doe	Jane	6/7/2009	6/7/2009 10:04 AM	6/7/2001	10:12 AM		8
				6/7/2009	10:23 AM	6/7/2009	11:00 AM		38
				6/7/2009	11:09 AM	6/7/2009	12:16 PM		67
				6/7/2009	12:16 PM	6/7/2009	12:22 PM		7
				6/7/2009	12:30 PM	6/7/2009	12:50 PM		20
				6/7/2009	1:41 PM	6/7/2009	1:41 PM		0
				6/7/2009	1:44 PM	6/7/2009	2:08 PM		24
				6/7/2009	2:10 PM	6/7/2009	2:18 PM		8
				6/7/2009	2:32 PM	6/7/2009	2:39 PM		7
						Daily Total:			179
				6/8/2009	6/8/2009 9:02 AM	6/8/2009	9:28 AM		26
				6/8/2009	9:46 AM	6/8/2009	9:46 AM		0
				6/8/2009	10:02 AM	6/8/2009	10:50 AM		48
				6/8/2009	12:54 PM	6/8/2009	1:46 PM		52
				6/8/2009	1:56 PM	6/8/2009	2:54 PM		58
						Daily Total:			184
				6/9/2009	6/9/2009 9:02 AM	6/9/2009	10:04 AM		63
				6/9/2009	10:20 AM	6/9/2009	10:50 AM		29
				6/9/2009	10:53 AM	6/9/2009	12:05 PM		73
				6/9/2009	12:19 PM	6/9/2009	1:03 PM		43
				6/9/2009	1:05 PM	6/9/2009	1:14 PM		9
				6/9/2009	1:15 PM	6/9/2009	1:50 PM		36
						Daily Total:			253

FIGURE 5.2. *A recreation of the Productivity Report.*

can see that the interpreter logged out at 1:41 P.M. and logged back in at 1:44 P.M. On the Log there would be a corresponding entry that would provide an explanation of the 3 minutes the interpreter was not "on call."

After the gaps in time on the Productivity Report are explained using the Log, the Productivity Report is then compared to another computer-generated document, which shows the number of minutes per log-in that an interpreter is connected to two callers. This other document is used to determine the minutes generated by the interpreter, or the "billable minutes." From this report, Ease Communication can determine each interpreter's actual productivity. The information in this report is aggregated, without the individuals' names, and sent to the National Exchange Carrier Association for reimbursement.

The log-in and log-out times are important but, as it was explained to me, the Daily Total minutes tallied on the Productivity Report, or the total number of minutes per shift the interpreter is "on call" and can be found, are really what management, internal and external to the center, look at for a productivity measurement. The Daily Minutes for each interpreter for a given month are combined and submitted, as I will discuss in the next section, to the National Exchange Carrier Association for reimbursement from the FCC. The rate at which minutes are reimbursed, has been set through negotiations among these bodies and companies such as Ease Communication, and it assumes that it is feasible for interpreters to spend about 38 percent of every hour actually doing interpreting. This percentage is therefore mandated by the National Exchange Carrier Association and closely monitored by Ease Communication.

During each hour, interpreters are required to be on the phones interpreting (producing billable minutes) for 24 minutes. Therefore, for an 8-hour shift, minus the half-hour lunch, interpreters should be available to take calls for approximately 180 minutes. When the interpreters are not interpreting for an average of 24 minutes per hour, they are considered to not be performing adequately. Using this report, the national office for Ease Communication can examine the actual minutes interpreted by each interpreter, and thereby determine if the interpreter is billable for 38 percent, or 24 minutes, of every hour.

The Productivity Report has two purposes within the center. It is used by management to document the number of minutes per shift an interpreter is logged into the system and available to accept calls. The second purpose is to check against the weekly invoice or timecard of each interpreter to ensure she is billing for the time she was actually on the phones, with the unavailable minutes documented in the Log.

The Productivity Report allows management to calculate, for a given time period, the number of minutes an interpreter is not logged into the phones. The Log can be used to explain discrepancies between the Productivity Report and the invoice submitted by the interpreter. It can also explain times when the interpreter is not billable. This prevents interpreters being penalized for being away from the phones for "acceptable" reasons. Nancy, the scheduler at one of the centers, told me:

> I look at the [Log] and then I compare it to their Productivity Report. If there is a time that [interpreters] are off the phones [which I can see from the Productivity Report] then they should have it documented on the [Log], most of the time they do. Sometimes they don't and I have to ask them what happened. But if it is there then I can just adjust their Productivity Report so they don't get into trouble.

If an interpreter is considered to be off the phones for an excessive amount of time, he could be approached by the manager and face sanctions; however, this is not Nancy's concern. When she says "get into trouble" she actually means that they need to be accountable:

Jeremy: Trouble?
Nancy: Well it isn't like they are going to get fired. I just mean that this way numbers look ok. If I didn't adjust [the numbers] then we wouldn't know why they weren't taking calls.

Furthermore, there are layers of accountability. That is, "the numbers" have to "look okay" to the managers, who can presumably show the numbers to their supervisors to demonstrate sound management over their center. In this way, the Productivity Report and Log are used to organize the work of interpreters and the work of their supervisors.

Managers may also rely on the Productivity Report to determine which shift an interpreter receives. Elizabeth, an interpreter who has worked for Ease Communication since it opened its center in her hometown nearly five years ago, told me that she was informed that the shifts are given based on efficiency, which is calculated using the Productivity Report. Even though Elizabeth was warned to "make her numbers," she has never heard of anyone not being allowed to work because of their Productivity Report:

> I know many interpreters who are never on the phone but they are still here. Also, I heard of one interpreter who got into trouble because he had really high numbers but they found out that he was really talking to his friends, not interpreting. I guess it doesn't matter because Ease Communication still gets paid.

Here, Elizabeth is talking about a rumor she heard about someone in her center who was said to have been making calls from his cellular phone to VRS and then placing outgoing calls on his videophone. There are a limited number of centers open twenty-four hours, and this interpreter was able to call through the relay number and get placed into his queue for his center. Apparently, he continued to do this until he received his own phone call. He would then call out on his videophone to his deaf friends and carry on conversations with them. The calls would be billable to the FCC because they would be connected to two different callers; therefore, Ease Communication would be reimbursed for the call even though this interpreter was not interpreting. Before this study was completed, several interpreters in different Ease Communication centers were fired for making fraudulent calls.

In addition to documenting productivity, interpreters' work must be made visible so Ease Communication can receive payment from the FCC through the National Exchange Carrier Association. At times, this aspect of the work frustrates some of the interpreters. Julia, for example, had worked for Ease Communication for six months before she decided to stop because she felt a conflict between the field of interpreting, which she sees as service driven, and Ease Communication, which is driven by the capacity "to make money." She expressed her frustration with the emphasis on numbers rather than effective interpretations:

> I hated the work. I hated it . . . I felt so schizophrenic. I had to be this and then be that. I was constantly being told not to do what I had been trained to do, as an interpreter. Don't deal with the language, deal with the mechanics. Don't be personable, be a robot. Don't deal with culture and language issues, just say the fucking thing and get your minutes counted so we can get paid by the FCC.

According to Elizabeth, the measurement of efficiency is a means by which Ease Communication rewards or penalizes interpreters by denying them their preferred shifts. As Julia points out, it is essential that Ease Communication be able to tally minutes for reimbursement and this can, at least in Julia's experience, create a stressful situation. This accounting method examines productivity in terms of dollars and cents rather than effectiveness. The goal of access then may begin to seem secondary, or even tertiary, to making money.

National Exchange Carrier Association

Interpreters are not the only ones who must be accountable. Although the reports are used internally to organize the work of interpreters, they are also used to produce external reports so that the Ease Communication can receive remuneration for their services and demonstrate that it is in compliance with the regulations established by various organizations. "At the interface between organizations, accounting categories work to align one organization's work processes with those of others (funders, creditors, customers)" (McCoy 1998, 396). I would now like to explore the funding entities that take up these reports and that are involved with the coordination of the work of sign language interpreters.

The name of the game is minutes; therefore, minutes have been made visible, measurable, and billable. Minutes represent what Espeland (1984) calls "commensuration—the transformation of different qualities into a common metric" (2). One of the consequences of commensuration is that "it can render some aspects of life invisible or irrelevant" (2). In 2006, all VRS providers combined reported 34,882,402 completed minutes between January and June. At a rate of approximately $6.64 per minute, the combined revenue earned for video relay for the same time period was

$231,619,149.28.[26] This is the amount that the FCC paid to VRS providers from revenue collected from the phone tax. Although this indicates that a lot of interpreting time has occurred, it does not show what actually happened. Nor does it show us if communication was successful.

The FCC establishes the rules that govern the provision of video relay services and determines the reimbursement rate; however, a third organization is brought into the mix to act as the payment center: the National Exchange Carrier Association, which is often referred to by its initials NECA (pronounced "necka"). The rate at which minutes are reimbursed by NECA has fluctuated since VRS was established. Originally, VRS providers were reimbursed approximately $18.00 per minute. This rate was dropped after a couple of years and has remained around $7.00 a minute. Jacob, an language interpreter who has worked in a variety of settings and now works for Ease Communication as a manager, explained that the initial fee paid to VRS providers was intended to cover the costs associated with establishing centers and training necessary staff. Since those initial costs are gone, the reimbursement was lowered. Jacob explains NECA's role:

> You see the National Exchange Carrier Association has financial responsibility. That means that when the money is collected from taxes [to pay for relay] that money is given to NECA. We then send NECA our monthly reports stating how many minutes we provided interpreting for. These reports also demonstrate that we are meeting the requirements set by the FCC.

NECA was established by the FCC in 1983 to perform telephone industry tariff filings and revenue distributions, following the breakup of AT&T.[27] It also has other functions, but in relation to VRS, NECA has become synonymous with measurements. Here, Jacob explains the formula that is used to measure efficiency:

> NECA is the number of minutes you are actually interpreting divided by number of minutes you are actually logged in. That means for every hour you are on the clock you should be interpreting for 24 minutes. That translates to 38 percent NECA. So you are working for 38 percent of every hour. The standard in the field of video relay is 38 percent.

26. http://www.neca.org/source/neca_resources_4438.asp (Retrieved 12/05/06).
27. http://www.neca.org/source/NECA_AboutUs_279.asp.

In this account, the abbreviation for the National Exchange Carrier Association, NECA, refers to the standards to which each interpreter is held. The formula that Jacob describes allows management to figure out each interpreter's productivity for a given time period.

Even though the rate is set by the FCC, the VRS providers are instrumental in how the rate gets determined, and they have a stake in keeping this number low—although they would never state it that way. This helps to keep the reimbursement at its current rate. Jacob explains:

> However, the industry realizes the importance of keeping the efficiency [numbers] low. Well, of course we are in it to make a profit, but at the same time if the efficiency rate gets too high then there will be a demand for interpreters to produce more minutes. Which means that repetitive motion injuries, carpal tunnel syndrome, emotional trauma that occur during calls, that interpreters do not experience out in the community, would increase. It would cause a lot of problems. In some ways efficiencies are kept artificially low to protect interpreters and to keep the reimbursement rate high.

Jacob's explanation demonstrates how management, as he sees it, takes seriously the interests and needs of the interpreters. To operate within these human limitations, VRS providers manipulate productivity numbers. To keep the efficiency rate artificially low, VRS providers might employ more trainee interpreters so that the more experienced interpreters are spending more time providing guidance to newer interpreters than they are actually processing calls. While these experienced interpreters are providing guidance to the newer interpreters, they are typically logged off of the system and unable to take calls. This means that Ease Communication and other VRS providers can point to the low number of calls being answered as a rationale for not raising the NECA.

Trainee interpreters are often those interpreters who do not hold a national certification. (Interpreters who are new to VRS but certified can also fall into this category.) As a result of not having a national certification, they are typically less likely to find employment through interpreter referral agencies that supply interpreters outside of VRS. They are also, on average, paid considerably less than a certified interpreter. While relying on noncertified interpreters to process calls, and using certified interpreters to provide guidance, does help reduce burnout and protects sign language interpreters from forms of repetitive motion trauma, it also creates a pool of VRS interpreters who, once trained, will be a cheaper form of labor for VRS providers. In addition, newer interpreters who lack experience may take longer to process the same call that a seasoned interpreter could do quickly. This is because a newer interpreter may require more clarification before providing an interpretation of a message. All the time the newer interpreter is getting clarification, they are able to bill the FCC. Accordingly, although Jacob suggests that Ease Communication is concerned about the interpreters' well-being, the company's decisions are also tied to potential earnings.

A focus on billable minutes can, at times, create confusion among the interpreters because they are unsure as to the priorities of the corporation. Estelle blames this confusion on a lack of understanding of the "corporate culture" of Ease Communication:

> The corporate culture . . . it isn't clear what Ease Communication wants from me as far as the corporate culture. Do they really want me to be efficient, hitting my targets, and I do hit all my numbers so that really isn't an issue. But let's suppose two or three years from now they want to up the ante like they want to increase their efficiency to 95 percent because [Ease Communication] wants to do better . . . Right now the pressure isn't on. What is the corporate culture you are trying to make? Do you want to be a company known for good customer service?

Like all of the interpreters I spoke with, Estelle understands that Ease Communication is a business. The goal of any business is to make money. However, Estelle suggests that the potential "corporate culture" of Ease Communication could be at odds with the work of interpreters and the provision of good service. Julia similarly perceived this, which drove her to stop working for Ease Communication. Although Estelle states that "now the pressure isn't on," having interpreters use the Log to document reasons for being off the phones so that productivity can be adjusted suggests that while the pressure may not be on, interpreters are made aware of the importance of their efficiency, and the Log could become a mechanism for increasing pressure in the future.

The interpreters I spoke with often blamed Ease Communication for the focus on numbers. It is easy to blame the person or organization you have daily contact with for changing what counts as productive. However, Ease Communication is merely establishing a protocol that can meet the requirements set by the FCC. Furthermore, some may assume that I am suggesting that prior to VRS the work of sign language interpreters was not textually organized. This would be a misinterpretation of my point. In fact, there are many other texts, such as various certifications, invoices, and the Code of Professional Conduct, to name a few, that have always organized and will always organize the work of interpreters. In my opinion, VRS provides an optimal site for exploration into how texts are used to organize sign language interpreters' work.

CONCLUSION

The term "functionally equivalent" is a product of the Americans with Disabilities Act and the practices put in place to ensure it as an outcome to connect people to a national discourse surrounding disability and equality. It moves beyond the immediate provision of any one service and connects different people providing different services to different people in different locales.

Although functional equivalency is the desired outcome set forth in the ADA, there is not one definition for it. That is, depending on the context (e.g., children's education, employment, VRS, etc.) the definition changes. However, what are the assumptions inherent in this institutional discourse across these various settings?

One assumption is that access can be quantified. And in order to quantify it, there must be a measure. That measure typically is the nondisabled body. However, Disability Studies scholars have encouraged us to move away from the essentialist "either/or" construction of ability and disability and discover ways in which people's differences are celebrated rather than objectified (Linton 1998; Davis 2002). Feminist scholars have also encouraged an analysis that takes into account the situated knowledges of various subjects (Harding 1997). In explicating the term "functional equivalency" we can see that the fight is far from over. Within this paradigm, access is reduced to a numeric representation of communication known as functional equivalency. What does not get calculated are the various forms of labor that deaf people and interpreters engage in as they attempt to receive and provide access.

The goal of VRS is to provide a telephone service for deaf people that is functionally equivalent to telephone services that non-deaf people enjoy. In an effort to accomplish this goal, people's individual preferences and experiences are set aside in order to produce measurable tallies. The particularities of an individual caller, such as unique signing style, are not part of the picture.

Texts are important tools used within the ruling relations in the organization of the everyday/everynight of people's lives. Traditionally, interpreters have been accountable to the deaf and non-deaf people with whom they were working. Within this new format, consumer feedback is secondary in the analysis of interpreters' accountability. Interpreters' primary responsibility is adherence to measurable outcomes that are devised and disseminated by extralocal organizations and operationalized through the use of texts.

Various texts are taken up and activated in VRS centers. From the Kudos Certificate to the Activity Log and Productivity Report, texts are a permanent feature of the provision of VRS. These texts are used to encourage certain behavior (e.g., the Kudos Certificate) and to discourage other behaviors (e.g., the Activity Log).

Sign language interpreters are made aware of the goal to be on the phone 38 percent of their time, but the purpose of the reports is often unclear. Some interpreters, such as Elizabeth, assume that Ease Communication uses the reports to reward and penalize interpreters. Others, such as Julia, tie the reports to capitalism, pure and simple.

These texts have an important role in organizing the work of interpreters in VRS. They focus on making call processing, rather than interpreting, the visible and measurable practice. What has not been accounted for is the ways in which our work is based on experience. Aspects of interpreters' work, such as language assessment and interpreting from one culture to another, remain invisible and unable to be measured and, therefore, they are not part of the calculations. Because the analysis is based on numbers, input from the consumers, both deaf people and non-deaf people, is secondary.

Although the time spent connected to both callers is used by the FCC and Ease Communication as a measurement of providing a functionally equivalent service, these organizations do not calculate whether or not the callers' needs were met during the call. Indeed, they are not required to. To help ensure quality (or at least give the appearance of paying attention to quality), Ease Communication instituted the Kudos Certificates. However, these certificates intended to encourage interpreters to provide quality to the VRS callers seem not to be taken seriously by interpreters or their managers.

In addition to demonstrating the ways in which the ruling relations are connected to VRS work, I have also shown how a new management of interpreting, which focuses on "more bang for the buck," employs technologies in an effort to create a functionally equivalent service. In doing so, this new system fails to recognize the effect of standardization on those who rely on sign language interpreting for access and those who see their craft as a professional skill.

In this chapter, I have focused only on those texts that were taken up or mentioned by the informants of this study. There are undoubtedly other texts that are used for billing NECA, disciplining interpreters, and demonstrating adherence to other federal regulatory bodies, such as the Occupational Safety and Health Administration (OSHA). Although I have not discussed all of these texts, I have attempted to show how the main accounting texts are taken up in this setting and beyond it as a replacement for the actual work of people.

As we move into the ruling apparatuses we see how the work of interpreters in VRS centers is taken up and transformed into a concept, "functional equivalency." Much like the work of social workers (see de Montigny 1995), the documentation does not account for the actual lived experiences of the users of VRS because they are not consulted. Instead, it is accountable to the "politico-administrative regime" (G. Smith 1995) that deaf people engage when they wish to place a phone call through VRS. Access, then, is defined not by interpreters' effectiveness, but by their ability to maintain a percentage.

Chapter 6

Connecting the Dots and

Pointing in New Directions

Throughout this book, I have explored the work of access. In doing so, I have demonstrated a sociology of interpreting. Following Smith (1987) and other institutional ethnographers, I began my study in the everyday of interpreters and moved into the ruling relations that interpreters organize and are organized by, examining various aspects of VRS: actors, environment, and the texts. I undertook this examination within the context of the professionalization of sign language interpreters and how this particular social organization affects the relationship between deaf people and interpreters. As I stated in the beginning, my goal was not to generalize the activities of the interpreters or deaf people to all interpreters or deaf people. Rather, my aim was to show the generalizing effect of the organization of VRS.

In chapter 2, I discussed the design of VRS call centers. The design is intended to produce a worker who is able to focus on her or his work and provide confidential interpretation for callers. Ease Communication has equipped each cubicle with the necessary technology and documents to enable interpreters to be self-sufficient workers. Along with the layout, I described the people one might encounter in a VRS center. In addition to being different from traditional, face-to-face sign language interpreting, VRS is an unusual setting for professional labor. While it depends on sophisticated broadband technologies, it also resembles the organization of lower-level service and telephone sales work that often occurs in call-center settings. This new medium for interpreting and the complex organization of which it is a part changes both the service interpreters can provide and also the nature of their work.

After providing the general layout, I focused on the primary users of VRS. In chapter 3, I discussed the data collected from two focus groups with deaf people. In particular, I focused on the calculated consumer labor that deaf people employ that enables them to gain access through VRS. This mostly invisible work is both a product of an inaccessible society and a dependence on another person for access. And, whereas the deaf users I spoke with praised this new service as providing them with improved access, they nevertheless used different strategies to accommodate the accommodation.

Deaf people often made a conscious effort to avoid confronting interpreters whom they felt were not providing adequate service. This decision, and others like it, have far-reaching implications. Deaf people typically have to struggle to gain access to the world in which they live. This struggle can mean that deaf people must be ready to attempt to read lips, write notes in their second language, or decipher gestures. It is understandable that there are times when deaf people would rather avoid the struggle by employing a nonconfrontational approach to getting access. However, although complaints can be emotionally draining endeavors, deaf people's reluctance to confront interpreters could be perceived as an endorsement of the caliber of services they are receiving. Their accounts in chapter 3 indicate that it is important to solicit their stories, outside of the immediate encounter, in order to determine how well they are being served by current practices.

In VRS, deaf people rely on interpreters so they can communicate over the phone. The interpreters, as I discussed in chapter 4, have to consider several factors when rendering an interpretation between two languages. The provision of VRS increases the factors that interpreters must consider, such as procedures that are dictated by corporate and governmental interests. Complying with governmental and corporate rules and regulations changes the relationship between interpreters and the deaf people with whom they work; it means that interpreters have less time than in face-to-face interpreting to ascertain their clients' particular needs and preferences as well as the context for the encounter. Interpreters in video relay must develop strategies for providing effective interpretation without having access to the context prior to the call.

Finally, in chapter 5 we saw that in addition to being accountable to rules and regulations put in place by the corporate and governmental bodies when doing video relay service work, VRS interpreters are also being held accountable to historical discourses about what it means to be disabled (Davis 1995). The standard by which access is understood is based on the non-deaf person's experience using the telephone. The FCC mandates that for users of VRS to achieve functional equivalency their experience using the telephone should mirror that of non-deaf people. Therefore the standard of measurement is the non-deaf experience. Using this standard reinforces the binary between disability and ability. These discourses are brought into the everyday/everynight practices of sign language interpreting through people activating various texts. Through these texts, interpreters' work is organized and connected to extralocal entities, such as the FCC and NECA.

Access, as the product of work, often goes to the highest bidder. This is often the case in a capitalist society. The aim of VRS and those who operate within the institution of access is to provide a service. Ideally, that service would be of high quality. However, there is yet to be a mechanism that is suitable for evaluating, in any measurable way, the efficacy of VRS. Therefore, most mechanisms must rely on a numerical system of evaluation.

Therefore, another way in which these texts organize the work of interpreters is by making their work measurable. The work of signed language interpreters is largely invisible. Often only the end product, the signed or spoken translation, is visible to noninterpreters. Now, interpreters' work is evaluated, primarily, on the number of billable minutes each interpreter is able to accrue during a shift. Whether the interpretation received by both callers was effective is a secondary consideration. Perhaps notions of "customer service" might provide a way of thinking more deeply about access, from the point of view of deaf people and their goals in using the telephone.

Most of the data presented in this book were collected over four years. The formal data collection process ended in 2007. In the two years since I began writing, the VRS industry has continued to change. More providers have opened; some have closed. Those that have remained open have continued to refine their policies, and sign language interpreters have begun to develop guidelines (e.g., Standard Practice Papers) for working in this particular setting. Moreover, as with any system, people have figured out ways to take advantage of its vulnerabilities.

In chapter 5, I mentioned that several interpreters were fired for making fraudulent calls. To my knowledge there were no criminal charges filed against any of these interpreters. Initially, it appeared that this was only a few rogue unscrupulous interpreters. However, on November 18, 2009, twenty-six people were indicted for conspiracy to defraud the United

States government.[28] (These individuals did not work for Ease Communication but for another provider.) Even before the indictments were handed down in November, the FBI had been interviewing interpreters, examining call records, and collecting office supplies from at least one video relay provider.

The indictments included six counts: Conspiracy to Defraud the United States and to Cause the Submission of False Claims, 18 U.S.C. § 371; Submission of False Claims, 19 U.S.C. §§ 287 and 2; Conspiracy to Commit Wire Fraud, 18 U.S.C. § 1349; Wire Fraud, 18 U.S.C. §§ 1343 and 2; and Criminal Forfeiture, 18 U.S.C. § 982. In short, a VRS provider conspired with other agencies and interpreters to make fraudulent calls using VRS that were then billed to NECA.

Many video relay providers have felt the effects of the indictments. In some cases, the FCC has refused to reimburse providers for conference calls in which deaf people participated, regardless of whether the calls were legitimate or not, because this was one of the ways that those indicted racked up billable minutes: Employees would hold weekly conference calls to discuss both business and leisure activities; because most, if not all, of the participants on the call were deaf, each called through a video relay interpreter. In other situations the provider would hire deaf people in the community to call into podcasts through VRS and sit on the line to increase billable minutes for the provider. It should be noted that although Ease Communication was not, to my knowledge, charged with anything, they did hire non-deaf, nonsigning customer service representatives, so deaf customers with issues for customer service had to call through VRS in order to gain access to customer service.

Although the case has not yet been decided, the action of the interpreters and the video relay providers deserves some attention. In some ways, the indictments against the twenty-six interpreters, the behavior of the interpreters at Ease Communication, and the practice of having deaf

28. See *United States of America v. Marc Velasquez Verson, Ellen Thompson, and Dorris Martinez; United States of America v. Benjamin Pena, Robert Z. Rubeck, and Tamara Frankel; United States of America v. Yosbel Buscaron, Lazaro Fernandez, Wanda Hutchinson, Jessica Bacallao, and Kathleen Valle; United States of America v. Irma Azrelyant, Joshua Finkle, Natan Zfati, Oksana Strusa, Alfia Iskandarova, and Hennadii Holovkin; United States of America v. Kim E. Hawkins, Larry Berke, Dary Berke, Lisa Goetz, and David Simmons; United States of America v. John T.C. Yeh, Joseph Yeh, Anthony Mowl, Donald Tropp, and Viable Communication, Inc.*

customers call through VRS to deal with a customer service representative highlights the vulnerability of this service, which has far-reaching implications. First and perhaps most important, if interpreters are "busy" processing fraudulent calls for the mere purpose of racking up billable minutes, then who is working with the actual consumers of the service? Presumably, there were fewer interpreters available to do the actual access that the VRS is intended to provide. This should be a primary concern.

Now, this could be seen as a product of the "corporate culture," as Estelle calls it. After all, if one interpreter decided to break the rules, one could easily argue that she was a bad seed. If the behavior was simply the "corporate culture," we would likely see it occur within only one provider. However, colleagues who have worked for a variety of providers have noticed these practices at different providers. When multiple people, in multiple locations, follow the same practices, the examination should explore something bigger than the individual actors. This does not excuse the behavior of interpreters or the indicted, but when the focus on productivity is on the ability to accrue billable minutes rather than quality of the service provided, then individuals work to maximize their billable minutes because this is the ideology within which they are working.

CONNECTING THE DOTS

This book has been an exploration into the work that goes into video relay service interpreting. My goal was to discover what is actually happening with the provision and use of video relay services. Throughout my exploration I have moved beyond the everyday/everynight lives of sign language interpreters and moved into what Dorothy Smith (2005) calls the "ruling relations."

The approach I chose to use—institutional ethnography—provided me with the "capacity to dissect the social organization of ordinary events through a research process of explication of the everyday world" (Rankin and Campbell 2006, 167). I began with the everyday practices of sign language interpreters who provide VRS interpreting. I wanted to understand how their work was organized and by whom.

Expanding Literature

This study contributes to three fields of scholarship. The first field is that of Disability Studies. Disability Studies scholars examine the disabling effect of a society that fails to appreciate differences. The second field is the field of sociology of work and the professions. I have employed a feminist use of the term "work," which is broadly defined (Smith 1988). In this way, I include a myriad of practices, paid and unpaid, that connect people through their actions. Finally, this research expands the literature within the field of sign language interpreting.

DISABILITY STUDIES

Disability Studies scholars take as one of their foci the power of definition (see Davis 2002; Ferri and Connor 2006).[29] Disability Studies examines not only how certain terms, such as *disability, impairment,* or *handicap* get defined, but also who has the power to create those definitions. My study also considers the significance of the power of definition. Of particular interest for me is how and by whom *access* gets defined. Throughout this book we have seen how the notion of access gets taken up legislatively, and in the regulations developed to implement legislation, such as the ADA.

This book demonstrates the ways in which access (and the information it can impart) becomes a "commodity" (Marx [1867]1976); as such, it is defined, organized, and sold by the government, businesses, and interpreters to the general population through phone taxes. Furthermore, functional equivalency becomes more than a measurement; it becomes a message about what is normal in society. Video relay service is evaluated on whether it is comparable to the services received by non-deaf persons rather than on whether it meets the needs of deaf people. Furthermore, this mode of evaluation presumes that there is one type of non-deaf person and that whatever that person expects, all deaf persons will expect. This does not take into account that it is this very practice that is disabling, not the reliance on the services of interpreters. Disability is the product of a society obsessed with categories. Although the idea of functional equivalency is taken from the ADA, the term has been taken out of context. That is, the entire Act intends, at least on its face, that access should be considered on a case-by-case basis (Rothstein 2002). Where the ADA has encouraged individuality, the FCC, in the way it implements and

29. A central theme in a Deaf Studies perspective is the cultural identities of people who see themselves as a linguistic minority, a theme which is often at odds with Disability Studies. Therefore, here I will focus on the implications of my work for Disability Studies and not Deaf Studies.

evaluates functional equivalency, has opted for a categorical approach to inclusion.

SOCIOLOGY OF WORK AND THE PROFESSIONS

In addition to adding to the field of Disability Studies, this study also takes up the issue of the changing nature of work. It is becoming more common for service providers to engage computer technologies when delivering services. In some cases, customers no longer engage another individual; instead they press various buttons on a computer screen to get their needs met. It is not uncommon to see individuals checking themselves out of stores, such as Home Depot or grocery stores. In fact, libraries across the United States now have a mechanism by which patrons can check out their own books. All of this points to the growing dependence on computer technology as part of the everyday.

This technology is often more convenient, but it also disengages people from each other. As we are trained as consumers and practitioners that engaging individuals is a slower, less efficient process, what does this mean for the desired professional status of practitioners? Work becomes less individualized and more organized by and dependent on computer programming. If we agree with the deprofessionalization thesis, the mere dependence on computer systems narrows the knowledge gap that sustains professional authority. However, even if we agree with Freidson (1994) that the knowledge gap is not narrowing, we must admit that a key component of professional status is functional autonomy. Thus, the growing regulation by computers and the focus on numbers as assessment tools may impede sign language interpreters' goal of becoming a recognized profession, particularly in this setting. Sign language interpreters could, as Peterson (forthcoming) suggests in his well-formulated argument, instead opt for the label of Communication Assistant (CA), like that of text-relay operators. However, this would merely accept the status quo as the optimum, rather than push for actual access.

Relationships

Perhaps most importantly, this study is about relationships. It is about the relationships between deaf people and interpreters, between interpreters and other interpreters, interpreters and management, and interpreters and organizations that are beyond the immediate environment that interpreters engage, sometimes without their knowledge. In comparison with face-to-face interpreting, VRS has brought several changes to the work of interpreters. In VRS, signed language interpreters are not permitted to converse with deaf callers before the start of the call. Interpreters are also interpreting more intimate conversations between deaf callers and those they are in relationships with or those they wish to be in relationships with. Finally, interpreters have become non-people. They are merely the "technology of voice" (Padden and Humphries 2005). These relationships inform other relationships.

The work of sign language interpreters is heavily dependent on the relationship they develop with deaf consumers, so it makes sense that "to encourage quality service work, service employees must look for management methods that deemphasize obtrusive managerial or bureaucratic control and give greater leeway to employees when working with customers" (Fuller and Smith 1996, 75). However, Ease Communication is at the mercy of federal regulations and fiduciary responsibilities. In order to adhere to the contract Ease Communication has entered into with the FCC, it must regulate interpreters in a visible way. This is why the "commensuration" is so important (Espeland and Stevens 1984). Through this tallying, recordkeeping, and reporting, VRS providers such as Ease Communication are able to continue to provide services to deaf and non-deaf people who wish to communicate with one another over the phone. Furthermore, just as interpreters work between two or more people, so does Ease Communication and other VRS providers. While they are responsible to the contracts they have with FCC, VRS providers are also responsible to the corporate bottom line.

POINTING IN NEW DIRECTIONS

All research has a purpose. The purpose of this research is to make visible various apparatuses that organize VRS interpreters' everyday labor. However, for this particular study, there is another purpose. I hope that this research provides some guidance to the field of sign language interpreting and the communities of deaf people who use their services. Sign language interpreters for too long have failed to clearly convey the interpreting processes to the users of their services. They have assumed that deaf people understood or would trust in the process. Now is the time that they must truly become allies with deaf people. Regardless of how one feels about interpreters being considered professionals or about VRS, it must be recognized that these two phenomena are interconnected and inevitably change the dynamics of the relationship between deaf people and interpreters.

As a service for their use, deaf people's understanding of how the provision of VRS changes and manages interpreters' work is extremely important. This can be understood as something beyond the provider, but explored as an institutional complex that situates deaf people as a homogeneous group. "Access" then is a set of practices, coordinated institutionally. It is more than a term, but an entire industry, ideology, and practice; it includes the various organizations, people, texts, and discourse taken up and put into place, all in an effort to allow deaf people to participate in the world they live in.

IMPLICATIONS AND FUTURE RESEARCH IN VRS AND BEYOND

Throughout this book, I have talked about the organization of the work of sign language interpreters, deaf people, and VRS providers. As I have talked about each of the stakeholders, I have examined the impact the work of interpreters has on them. Of course, I did not answer every question about VRS.

Deaf People

From a Disability Studies perspective, as the practice of interpreting changes in light of this new organization and interpreters work towards achieving professionalization, one of the concerns is how deaf people can remain a part of this organization. One of the significant impacts of VRS to the service deaf people receive is that there is less opportunity for interpreters to become familiar and comfortable with the various signing styles interpreters come in contact with daily. This means that there may be an increase in misinterpretations. This situation is exacerbated because increasing numbers of interpreters are working in VRS with little or no experience outside of VRS. In his study of face-to-face interpretation, Cokely (1992) suggested that to curtail the number of misunderstandings by interpreters "it would seem appropriate for [deaf] consumers to phrase salient and crucial portions of their discourse clearly and unambiguously" (163). While in everyday interactions this might be possible, in more volatile situations, it might not be reasonable or possible for a deaf consumer to remember to make accommodations for the interpreter. Furthermore, this does not solve the problem; it only shifts the responsibility for making accommodations from the VRS providers and interpreters to deaf people. Deaf people are typically the ones with the least amount of power. Deaf people should be clear when they sign, just like someone who is speaking should clearly articulate her or his speech. However, in some cases a more clearly signing deaf person is not going to increase the accuracy of the interpretation.

Another consideration for deaf people is the long-term impact of the fees paid to VRS interpreters. There is a shortage of signed language interpreters. While the increase in pay initiated by VRS will surely attract more potential interpreters, it also could eventually make access too costly for certain people. Historically, agencies and interpreters have struggled to get their relatively low fees paid (Bailey 2005). Small companies can argue that the cost of an interpreter is prohibitive and creates an "undue hardship," which would give them a clear exemption to providing accommodation under the ADA. VRS is able to pay considerably more to interpreters in part because they are subsidized by the state. One of the benefits of this subsidy is that interpreters were eager to work for VRS providers because they were able to earn more money. However, this leads to more money outside of VRS, as well. Since the start of VRS, there has been an average increase of $10 per hour for sign language interpreting services; in some cases, the pay has increased by $20. There will likely be no more such dramatic increases. However, when agencies that coordinate interpreting services factor in overhead costs, companies hiring interpreters could be asked to pay $75 to $100 an hour with a two-hour minimum. Large corporations may not experience any problem with such fees, but smaller companies that only need an interpreter for fifteen minutes may argue that it is unreasonable to pay such a fee. Companies claiming an "undue hardship" may find sympathy with the courts.

Signed Language Interpreters

VRS introduces a third component to an already complicated process: the computer equipment. The involvement of computer technology not only has implications for the multitasking capabilities of the interpreter, but it also influences the way in which language is produced and received. Linguistic anthropologists have already begun to look at the impact of computer-mediated communication. Keating and Mirus (2003) found that deaf people who use video cameras to communicate in sign language over the internet "alter[ed] their production of signs in the new context, and not just the relationship among their bodies, the camera, and the computer environment" (703). The requirements to be a signed language interpreter in a VRS center are being lowered. It is more common to see interpreters who have little experience outside of the VRS environment working in centers. Given that language is being affected, one must question the impact on new interpreters.

This brings me to the next possibility for future research: exploring the role of Certified Deaf Interpreters (CDIs) in the processing of video relay calls. CDIs are deaf people who are trained in ASL, English, and interpreting. Often these interpreters work with a non-deaf interpreter when the language of the deaf consumer is "esoteric to non-deaf interpreters in that region" (Stewart, Schein, and Cartwright 1998, 106). Because interpreting in VRS centers does not provide for interpreters getting to know the deaf person before the call begins, the use of CDIs would be ideal. Some centers that are fortunate enough to have trained deaf people in other roles working there have the benefit of this added component for access for callers. However, these centers are few in number.

To address these two implications, interpreters should begin to demand higher standards for working in VRS centers. They should not allow the success of their work to be determined by an ambiguous term like *functional equivalency*. They need to recognize that their ability to comprehend a 3-D language over a 2-D medium is limited. A way to assist with that is to ask for the assistance of a person who has grown up with the language and uses it every day to engage the world. These people should be trained interpreters who have a unique grasp on ASL and understand the process of interpreting and VRS.

Furthermore, interpreters should encourage VRS providers to employ the highest quality of interpreters. Although mentoring new interpreters is beneficial to the longevity and success of the field, there are limits to where these new interpreters should work. Interpreters are not doing a service to deaf or non-deaf people who use them if they do not demand quality practitioners.

Never before have signed language interpreters been the focus of mass recruitment in the way they have been since VRS began. Different companies are vying for their services. This places them in a very advantageous position, one they should attempt to capitalize on.

There is no doubt that VRS is shaping the field of sign language interpreting. As VRS has become a staple of the interpreting industry, there is a greater need for interpreters who are VRS ready upon graduating from interpreter preparation programs. There is also a need for more interpreters who possess national certification through RID. Yet interpreters who are attracted to VRS work and seek training for it must be cautious. In 2006, the president of RID, Angela Jones, accepted a $50,000 donation from one video relay provider to "support interpreter training, certification, and testing efforts" (Jones 2006, 5). VRS providers also sponsor national conferences on interpreting (VIEWS 2007). Although this money is used to offset the cost of those in attendance and reduce turnaround time for certification evaluations, it should be understood that such endeavors are not purely altruistic on the part of these providers. They are, in reality, special interest groups who are lobbying (Klein 2000).

Although the money most definitely does not come with explicit strings, an internalization process occurs. As RID is the interpreter certifying body in the United States, it behooves VRS providers to fill its treasury. The goal of RID is to certify qualified interpreters. The goal of VRS providers is to have interpreters to interpret calls so they are in compliance with the FCC's mandates and can continue to earn money. It is not unrealistic to question whether, eventually, RID's goal of quality will be at odds with VRS providers' goal of billable minutes. Once their money has been accepted, do interpreters become beholden to the providers' needs?

Furthermore, members of RID work for various VRS providers. They also serve on RID's board of directors as well as on advisory committees appointed by the board. I do not mean to imply any nefarious motives on the part of either party; nevertheless, these appointments muddy the water and call into question where loyalties lie. Furthermore, just as some VRS providers do not feel interpreters can be trusted to work for multiple providers and thus require a "do not compete clause" so too should interpreters question perceived conflict of interest in which they now find themselves.

VRS Providers

Many of the interpreters and some of the deaf people I spoke with throughout this study were quick to blame VRS providers for the rules and regulations that appear to be the cause for difficulties in their interactions. I have to admit that I originally assumed that the VRS providers were more interested in earning money than they were with providing quality service to deaf people. However, this study demonstrates that VRS providers are a small component of a larger organizational complex that spans multiple sites.

In some ways, the blaming of VRS is largely of their own making. VRS providers have done little to keep interpreters informed of the process by which rules and regulations get established. With the exception of sending out mass emails to encourage interpreters to write the FCC when they are discussing lowering the reimbursement rate for VRS calls, providers have kept interpreters and deaf people in the dark. I would encourage providers to establish a forum composed of deaf people and interpreters so that they are able to become informed and then educate more people about the processes. Furthermore, VRS providers should work with interpreters to find out how to begin to count and evaluate what interpreters consider to be important components of their work.

In addition to keeping deaf people and interpreters informed, it would behoove VRS providers to embrace the work of Dean and Pollard (2006), who encourage a supervision component in professional practice, so that interpreters are able to dialogue about their experiences and use the information gathered to improve their work. This supervision component would be comparable to that of medical students or other types of apprentices.

Providers should begin to lobby the FCC to allow for a mechanism that can account for the invisible work that deaf people and interpreters perform. The official record calculates minutes and those who read them define those minutes as access. However, through discussions with interpreters and deaf people, it becomes clear that there is much more to gaining and providing access. This requires that sign language interpreters and deaf people perform additional recognized and unrecognized labor that may be difficult to measure precisely but that may be key to providing and gaining access.

FINAL WORDS

In the beginning of this book, I stated that I have relied on my own experiences as a sign language interpreter, my training as a sociologist, and the "work knowledge" (D. Smith 2005) of those who participated in this study as an entry point into the ruling relations that organize the work of sign language interpreters who work in Ease Communication VRS centers. I will not pretend to suggest that I have told the entire story. What I have done here is demonstrated that the access gained through VRS is not the product of one person's, or even one group's, labor. And I have pulled on a strand of a larger ball of yarn that connects VRS work with notions of disability, occupational hierarchies, and capitalism.

In the first chapter, I recounted a story of the events that occurred at the 2001 Conference of the Registry of Interpreters for the Deaf in Orlando, Fla. I would like to begin this final section with a story from a more recent conference. The conference was the 2007 Conference of the Registry of Interpreters for the Deaf held in San Francisco, Calif. The opening ceremony, I believe, provides the perfect conclusion for this book.

During the opening ceremony, RID's board of directors thanked the numerous organizations that provided financial support for the conference. These organizations were, in large part, VRS providers. While I realize it is important to be gracious for, in some cases, tens of thousands of dollars given to my professional organization, I also thought that our gratitude was evident in the multiple banners that covered the walls of the conference hall recognizing the various organizations.

When each provider was recognized for their contribution to the organization ("Premium," "Platinum," etc.), a representative was invited to provide a speech. While each provider was presented with a heartfelt thank you and applause from the audience, I could not help but contemplate that interpreters have become a sought-after commodity. In the few minutes that each provider accepted thanks, they also made a plug for their company. One representative discussed how her company shared values, such as excellence, with RID. The speeches were pretty similar; however, there were two presenters whose closings caught my attention.

At the end of one speech, the provider's representative announced, "By the way, we do not have a do-not-compete clause." The crowd went wild. Interpreters hooted and hollered their support for the organization that would not require interpreters to sign a do-not-compete clause. This would allow interpreters not to have to wait for one year after leaving one VRS provider before joining another provider. Immediately following this frenzy of excitement, a provider that did require interpreters to sign a do-not-compete clause was recognized for their contribution to RID. The representative, also wanting to end on a high note, in a gesture that was strangely reminiscent of a Clearing House Sweepstake winner's commercial, presented RID with an Ed McMahon–size check in the amount of $25,000. This gesture did not receive the same amount of jubilation from the audience. Some people did clap, but far fewer. This incident is illustrative of the choices practitioners of the field of interpreting must consider.

Although this study looked at VRS, I maintain that the same approach could be used to explore other venues in which sign language interpreters find themselves. There will be different actors, different expectations, and different texts to organize the work, but the same principle holds true: the work of sign language interpreters is being organized by extralocal apparatuses.

The work of sign language interpreting is changing. Interpreters are no longer solely responsible to their interpretation. In VRS, ensuring that the people they work with are able to fully participate in a given interaction is not interpreters' only responsibility. Interpreters must begin to have a fuller appreciation of what it means to be a representative for a company. They must recognize that contracts, which were not analyzed here, are not only used to secure their fee for services but also to prevent them from working for multiple venders. This type of work limits their ability to be effective interpreters. They have to discern what that will mean for themselves, as part of a field, and for their consumers. They should work to chart a course that will not only protect their own professional interests, but also expand the meaning of access for deaf people in a non-deaf world. And this, of course, requires more work.

Appendix A

Methods and Procedures

From the beginning, I conceptualized this project as an institutional ethnography. I wanted to explicate "the way things work" (DeVault and McCoy 2002) in the provision of VRS interpreting. This knowledge would allow me to understand how the work of sign language interpreters who work in video relay centers gets organized and by whom. Institutional ethnography provides a framework that focuses on people without making them the subjects of the study. It allows for an exploration into the larger social structures that coordinate the everyday lives of people.

Dorothy Smith (2005) has described institutional ethnography "as an alternative sociology, not as a methodology" (50). However, it is a way of orienting the researcher to their project; therefore I chose to discuss it in this section. Along with a brief discussion of institutional ethnography, I provide an account of the procedures I undertook to complete this study. I conclude this appendix with a discussion of the some of the characteristics of my study that I found significant.

INSTITUTIONAL ETHNOGRAPHY

In chapter 1, I introduced the topic of institutional ethnography as a way to situate myself in relation to this study. I talked about how institutional ethnographers begin with a problematic and, as with a ball of yarn, pull the string to unravel how things get done as they do. In what follows, I expound on this approach.

Drawing on ethnomethodology, phenomenology, and materialism, Dorothy Smith introduced institutional ethnography as a "feminist sociology" (1987). The goal is to use the expertise of people to explore the coordinating practices that occur beyond their everyday/everynight experiences (D. Smith 2005). With the recognition that people are active participants in the creation and maintenance of the social world, institutional ethnographers set out to explore how activities are coordinated across locales. This means that researchers explore "how [phenomena known to sociology] are organized as social relations, indeed as a complex of social relations beyond the scope of any one individual's experience" (D. Smith 1987, 151).

Institutional ethnographies provide a "map" (DeVault and McCoy 2002; D. Smith 2005) that shows how people's activities in different locations are connected to one another. These maps can be figurative or literal. I found that creating a literal map of the processes involved in providing interpreting in VRS helped me to focus in on those areas where my work and that of others moved beyond the walls of the center. Additionally, it allowed me to pinpoint places in the process where texts were invoked. My sketch, which represented only a portion of the steps in the process, illustrated that the process involves various people, in various locales, performing visible and invisible work. The visible work includes placing the call and interacting with the computer equipment. The invisible work includes the decision making that callers and interpreters do that is intended to improve access for the callers.

The various steps and activities are labeled, by the people who work in VRS, as call processing, call management, compliance, or interpreting. However, these categories are abstract. Often people's activities are discussed using institutional discourses that mask what is actually happening (D. Smith 2005). Hiring a sign language interpreter, providing a ramp for people who use wheelchairs, or providing communication boards for people with autism all get categorized as providing "access." Part of the goal of institutional ethnography is to look beyond the institutional discourse and show what actually happens.

Avoiding the institutional discourse does not mean that it is not important. In fact, there is recognition that the assertion made by poststructuralists/postmodernists that discourse has an organizing effect (Foucault 1972) is not completely wrong. However, in the ontology of institutional ethnography, researchers must remember that discourse is the product of people's doing. Therefore, an investigation of where discourse originated is necessary (D. Smith 1999). In this project, I view terms like *access* as discursive products that must be unpacked to be understood. To do this, I started with my own experience and the experiences of my colleagues. By talking with people who provide VRS, I come to understand what it is they do and why they do it.

Using institutional ethnography, the everyday/everynight work of sign language interpreters in VRS centers provides an entry into understanding and documenting how access gets defined. As an institutional ethnographer, I was guided by questions such as (a) How do interpreters get scheduled for shifts? (b) Who decides which interpreter gets which shift? (c) What texts are invoked or referenced as interpreters perform their work? (d) How do these decisions and practices get understood by VRS actors? Exploring these issues allowed me to explicate the extralocal ruling relations that coordinate the practice of sign language interpreting in VRS settings.

In examining "how things work," I used participant observations, texts, and interviews with people who participate in the process. These people are not the focal point of the examination. The goal is not to develop a grand theory in which the lives of people can be compartmentalized, but to understand the processes in which they participate. The people who share their reflexive accounts are experts. They know their lives and their collaboration with institutional ethnographers allows us to know how those lives are organized.

I set out to explicate the ruling relations that coordinate the work of sign language interpreters in the provision of VRS. I began, as institutional ethnographers do, with a problematic (see D. Smith 1987, 1990a; DeVault and McCoy 2002; Campbell and Gregor 2002). To explore my problematic, I chose four data collection methods: participant observation, interviews, focus groups, and analysis of texts. Below, I discuss the challenges—some standard, others unique—of each of the methods and how each allowed me to unpack and understand the practices that organize the work of sign language interpreters in the provision of VRS.

This approach differs from traditional sociology in that traditional sociology remains unaware that it too is a part of the social structure that it claims to be studying. Traditional sociologists begin with a theory and work to prove or disprove it. In institutional ethnography, the researcher starts by talking with people, whose accounts provide the entry into how things get done as they do.

I began by talking with sign language interpreters about our work in VRS. We talked about how our work was different from in-person interpreting and explored reasons for those differences. I listened for ways in which the stories of my colleagues, and my own experiences, implied a connection with "ruling relations" outside of VRS (D. Smith 2005). Thus, this is not a study of sign language interpreters and their consumers: deaf people and non-deaf people. Rather it is study of one aspect of the institution of access in which sign language interpreters, deaf people, non-deaf people, governmental agencies, corporations, and policies intersect.

As an institutional ethnography, this inquiry begins with an examination of activities of sign language interpreters. I was not attempting to develop or test a theory to explain the events I was seeing and hearing about. Rather, I would explicate these accounts and show them as they are (Rankin and Campbell 2006). The goal here was to "explain to people the social—or society—as it enters into and shapes their lives and activities" (D. Smith 1999, 97).

The data collected are based on experience. I have used my own experience during the participant observations; I also used the experience of deaf people and interpreters during the focus groups and interviews. This practice keeps the participant as an integral part of the study while making invisible practices visible to those who contribute to the organization.

Experiences, including my own, are fundamental to the exploration of the ruling apparatuses that organize sign language interpreters' lives (D. Smith 2006). During the interviews and my own work in video relay centers, texts were mentioned as having a role in VRS. The texts mentioned and discovered provided directions for further investigation. Through texts, people's activities can be standardized and organized across multiple locales. They provide further information about how experiences are shaped.

Informants

The people who participated in the study did much more than inform. They lent their expertise as practitioners, managers, and consumers of VRS to me. They were actually collaborators with me. Each person was asked to provide a pseudonym. In some cases when people could not think of one, they would charge me with coming up with one for them. At times the informants would mention another person during their discussions with me. To promote the free flow of information during the interviews, I changed these names during the transcription process.

DEAF COLLABORATORS

Of the six deaf people who participated in the focus groups, only one of them was a woman and one of them was Latino; the rest were white men. Although two of them stated they could hear a little with the use of hearing aids, all of them stated that their hearing loss was prelingual—that is, that their hearing loss occurred before they were able to speak. Three of them had deaf siblings or deaf parents. All of them had attended a school for deaf children for at least part of their primary education, and three had also attended Gallaudet University for some or all of their college education. All of them stated that ASL was their preferred method of communication. The ages of the deaf collaborators ranged from 35 to 81 years of age.

In addition to the deaf informants, I interviewed twenty-one sign language interpreters. All held at least one certification (e.g., NIC, CI, CT, or CSC) from the Registry of Interpreters for the Deaf. The average age of the participants was 39. All of the informants had a minimum of six months experience working in VRS. The informants cited life experience, religious affiliations, and interpreter training programs as ways they had learned their craft. Less than half of the interpreters were freelancers who contracted with Ease Communication; the rest were full-time paid staff in the organization. With the exception of one individual, all of the informants held at least an Associate of Arts degree. Only four held graduate degrees, two of which were in interpreting. Of the twenty-one interpreters I interviewed, four held management positions in VRS.

OTHER PERSONNEL

I was also able to talk to a scheduler for one of the centers. The scheduler was not an interpreter and did not know any sign language. At the time of the interview, the scheduler had worked for Ease Communication for little more than a year.

The Sites

There are two different sites from which the data for this study were collected. Both are operated by Ease Communication, which is one of fourteen corporations providing interpreting through VRS in the United States. Some video relay providers have video relay centers in Canada, but they still receive reimbursement from the FCC; therefore, at least one of the callers must be located in the United States so the video relay provider is able to receive remuneration.

The first site where I conducted participant observation is in Arizona. I knew most of the interpreters who worked in the center, either casually or as close friends. That is, I had worked with many of the interpreters over the years and had become quite fond of them and respected their work.

Others were former students whom I had taught in the local interpreter training program. Still others, mostly those who had recently relocated to the southwest or recently graduated from the local interpreter training program, I had only begun to know.

The site is laid out in a call center fashion. There are fourteen cubicles that are used by sign language interpreters to interpret calls and they are separated by high walls to prevent eavesdropping by other interpreters, although some interpreters mentioned how certain interpreter's voices would carry throughout the entire center. I had also experienced hearing some of my colleagues as they interpreted in cubicles next to me.

This center is located in a diverse metropolitan area in the state of Arizona with a large deaf community, within two hours of a residential school for deaf children and within one hour of a day school for deaf children. There are currently 159 sign language interpreters (109 certified and 50 noncertified) registered with RID who live in the state of Arizona.[30] I was unable to learn the exact number of interpreters who work for the center because the director considered that information proprietary. I do know, from my own work in the center and counting the number of mailboxes, that over one hundred interpreters provided interpreting for the center at different times. Arizona also has two interpreting preparation programs and a four-year Deaf Studies program housed at a state university. Currently there are two video relay providers in the state of Arizona and one of them has a satellite office.

The second center, which is laid out similarly to the first but has nearly twice the number of stations, including stations used by the manager and the scheduler, is located in upstate New York. It is located in a city with a large deaf community. This center is located within a few miles of the National Technical Institute for the Deaf (NTID) and multiple referral agencies. In addition to the numerous programs for deaf and hard of hearing students, NTID has an interpreter training program. There are approximately 442 sign language interpreters (149 certified and 293 non-certified) in the state of New York. However, it should be noted here that not all of these interpreters are in upstate New York; a large percentage live in and around New York City. When I spoke with the manager of the center, I was informed that there were approximately 80 interpreters

30. There may be more who chose, for a variety of reasons, not to become members of RID and therefore would not be included in this number but still practice the art and science of sign language interpreting.

registered to work in the center. However, most of them only worked weekends because they work full time at NTID. Upstate New York has two VRS providers and several interpreter referral agencies.

Participant Observation

A great deal about the ways in which people's lives are organized can be understood through observation. The way a person stands in relation to another, eye gazes, and body movements are just some communication strategies people use when interacting with each other. Observing people interact with each other, as researchers do in participant observation, allows researchers to see those being observed engage in what Goffman (1963b) calls "copresence." I watched the behaviors of people in the centers unfold with great interest. They provided insight into the relations that are at play within the VRS setting. Although it is ideal for participant observers to take a passive role during the first few days in the field (Taylor and Bogdan 1998), the field in which I carried out this study is one with which I am intimately familiar, having also provided sign language interpreting services within this setting. Therefore, a solely observational role was not practical.

GAINING ACCESS

To gain access to the first center, I contacted the director of the center in Arizona, where I had provided interpreting, via e-mail, and asked if I would be able to conduct my research at the center. The director only asked that I create a summary of my research so that it could be shown to the administration. My first challenge then was to write up a benign description of a study that aimed at being informative and critical simultaneously (see Appendix B).

Prior to writing the explanation, I had a phone conversation with the director. I used this time to answer any questions she may have had so that I could address them in the explanation. I was immediately surprised by the lack of concern for the confidentiality of the callers. Instead, the director was more concerned with proprietary information. However, she seemed to be put at ease when I explained that the technology was not the focus of my study. I also explained that I would refer to the provider she worked for only by a pseudonym.

Gaining access in the second center did not require any discussion with the director. Once she knew I already had permission from another center, she asked only where she needed to sign. Although I still presented her with a summary of the research, she did not read it and did not keep a copy.

DATA GATHERED

While in these locations, I observed various people carry out their duties in the centers. These people included the managers, directors, schedulers, and the interpreters. I sat with managers and the schedulers while they performed their duties of coordinating interpreters in order to better understand and map how it is that interpreters came to be assigned particular schedules/shifts. From the participant observations, opportunities arose to talk informally with the individuals I was observing.

Observations occurred spontaneously in the beginning. As I became more familiar with the setting and practices, observations became focused. At the first center, I worked for the month of July from 2003 to 2005, putting in eight and a half hours a day, Monday through Friday. From 2006 to 2007, I worked the "graveyard shift" from 11:00 P.M. to 7:00 A.M. during the month of July. I occasionally worked in other centers for Ease Communication during various weekends for training. I also worked approximately twenty hours a week at the second center from March 2006 to August 2007.

When I was not interpreting, I observed and collected data. To accomplish this, I spent time in the site when I was not scheduled to provide services and gathered data. When I was able, I attended staff meetings and trainings at both centers. The most beneficial data gathered were those I was able to gather while on breaks. I would sit in the break rooms at both centers and joined people outside while they smoked and talked about our work.

During the first few weeks, I walked around with my jotting pad. I found that people were self-conscious about what I was writing. Therefore, I did not bring my jotting pad on breaks with me. All of the interpreters knew I was conducting research and even asked me "Are you going to include our discussions in your study?" Still, they were more at ease and the conversations flowed more spontaneously when I stopped bringing my jotting pad. Therefore, as soon as the break was over, I would make notes into my notebook before I logged back into the system and starting taking calls. I would then use these notes to write memos as soon as my shift ended. As I mentioned before, for privacy reasons, I did not observe interpreters while they were interpreting calls.

The data I collected during my participant observation were invaluable. The participant observations allowed me to see how interpreters engaged one another in the common spaces, such as the break rooms. My observations also showed me about the rules of claiming space. I also came to realize the significance of the various texts. During my participant observations, I became aware of the various organizations that influence the practice of interpreting in this particular setting. Perhaps most importantly, I used this time to discern from the interpreters and management what they saw as significant in their everyday work.

This was not a covert research study. Individuals were made aware through spoken or signed language of the purpose of my presence. Individuals who wished to abstain from participation were not included in the analysis. Each person was asked if she or he was willing to participate and provided with two Informed Consent forms (see Appendixes C and D). Those who were willing to participate in the study were asked to sign one and give it back to me and keep the other one for their records. The Informed Consent has the number for the Institutional Review Board at Syracuse University, my phone number and e-mail, as well as the phone number of my dissertation supervisor, Professor Marjorie DeVault.

Interviews

Participant observations yield a great deal of data; however, the goal of institutional ethnography is to understand "how things work." The goal of this study is to understand these processes from a particular location (Collins 1986; Haraway 1988; Mann and Kelley 1997): that of sign language interpreters. Most institutional ethnographers do not rely solely on observations to gather data. They rely on the informants who lend their expertise to the explorations of the everyday worlds. Through interviewing, the researcher can get, from the informants, the view of their everyday/everynight lives. Interviewing allows the informants to be collaborators in the project rather than subjects.

Before I began interviewing and while I was working at Ease Communication, I talked informally with various interpreters about their work. Although I did not record (i.e., videotape or audiotape), I did make jottings immediately after the interactions, which provided a lot of insight and direction for this study. These spontaneous interactions allowed me to hear about different issues relevant to the interpreters and provided guidance for questions to use during the formal interviews. They also provided great stories about the work people are doing in video relay centers. Each of the informants was asked to provide a pseudonym that would be used throughout the study.

Interviewing has traditionally been used as a means of gathering personal narratives of informants. I used interviews to identify the components of the institutional complex and the influence they exert over informants' lives. To identify these parts, the interviews revolve around work. Defining work broadly, like feminist scholars do (D. Smith 1990a; Daniels 1987; DeVault 1991), also brings into focus those activities that are often unrecognized by the power structures but are required to allow recognized and paid labor to occur. Through discussions with informants about work, I learned about remote institutions and their role in the lives of signed language interpreters (DeVault and McCoy 2002).

The directors gave me permission to conduct my study at their centers. However, I still needed participants. Once I received permission from the director, I needed to gain what Leo (1995) calls "secondary access." This required that I contact interpreters. Since the first site was located in another state and I did not know all of the interpreters or when they were working, I was unable to call them. Instead, I drafted another letter. The second letter (see Appendix E) was addressed to my colleagues in the center and still had to be approved by the director. After it was approved, I sent the letter to a colleague in the center who placed a copy of the letter in each interpreter's mailbox. I was able to use the same letter, with slight modifications, in recruiting informants for the second site. In that case, I simply made copies and placed them in my colleagues' mailboxes when I worked at the center.

Approximately ten interpreters responded to my letters. These responses came in the form of e-mails or phone calls. Some waited until I arrived at the site and contacted me while I was working. Still more contacted friends of mine who worked at the site and told them they would like to participate in my study.

In addition to the letters, while I was working at both centers, I would occasionally send messages, either e-mails or instant messages, to my colleagues who were working with me and ask them to participate in the study. With the exception of two interpreters, everyone I made direct contact with was eager to help. Both of the individuals who did not participate in the study were from the center in Arizona. The first person who declined did not provide a reason. The second person's schedule did not permit a time for us to meet for an interview.

Interviews were scheduled to accommodate the schedules of the informants. Some of my informants had children so interviews were scheduled on multiple days. One of the centers remained open twenty-four hours a day and supervisors and schedulers left around 5:00 P.M. Therefore, some interviews occurred at the center in the conference room or break room after management had left. In one case, the interpreter was not able to participate in the interview before his shift began so I interviewed him at 12:30 A.M. after his shift was done.

With the exception of the interview with the scheduler, all of the interviews were videotaped to enable me to capture moments when participants chose to provide their answers in ASL. Although these interpreters can hear, it is not uncommon for them to code-switch between ASL and English to convey a more visual concept or one that may be difficult to express in English.

I prepared a list of open-ended questions to provide some structure to the interviews (see Appendix F). As often is the case with this type of project, I did not stick closely to the interview guide. I began each interview with questions about the individual's background and reasons for entering the field and then asked them to talk to me about interpreting for VRS. Then, I allowed the participant's answers to guide the process. Often, without probing from me, the participant would address each of my questions and more while they were telling me about their experience working in video relay. The interviews lasted anywhere from one and a half to two hours.

During the interviews, and later during the coding of the interviews, I was "searching for traces of how the participants' actions and talk [were] conditioned" (Campbell 1998, 60). I was particularly interested in identifying instances when the informants talked about or referred to institutional processes to which they were held accountable. My goal was to identify and explicate spaces where work, broadly defined, was coordinated.

Once I transcribed the interviews from the videotapes, I performed open coding on each interview. As I read through each line of the interview, I attempted to see the various types of work being done, by whom, and why. I then did focused coding (Emerson, Fretz, and Shaw 1995). The focused coding was used to hone in on the more specific details of what was being talked about in the transcripts.

When I was done with the focused coding, I cut and pasted the coded materials into different Word documents. I then printed them all out and cut the printed papers into sections with one piece of the transcript and its corresponding code on each strip of paper. I then spread them all out on my dining room table and attempted to lump the codes together. As I did this, themes and subthemes began to emerge. Some codes were changed into completely new codes and others were removed completely. When I was done with my focused coding, I began to produce memos for the codes. In these memos, I placed codes and quotes together and made notes about my thinking about the code and how it connected to the larger project.

Focus Groups

I had initially believed that I would only conduct interviews with those who worked in the centers. These people would include interpreters, managers, directors, and schedulers. The data collected from the interviews would lead to various texts that would connect the everyday practices of interpreters' work with the ruling relations that organize that work.

In 2005, at a conference at the University of Connecticut, I spoke about my project to a group. As the moderator for the session, Dorothy Smith asked me where the deaf people who use VRS were. This was not the first time the issue of deaf people and their participation in my project was discussed. In fact, in a writing group with my dissertation advisor and several of her advisees, the question was posed to me several times. I was a little hesitant to include that perspective because I thought it would change the focus of my project. And, honestly, I wasn't sure how I was going to go about including deaf people. Luckily, I did not have to figure it out alone. During the defense of my proposal the question was raised again. My committee suggested I conduct focus groups.

Therefore, in addition to the interviews with managers, directors, schedulers, and interpreters, I held a focus group in each state. I invited six people to each focus group. However, only two individuals showed up for the focus group in upstate New York. For the focus group in Arizona, four people participated.

These focus groups provided a great deal of insight into the experience and work of deaf people as they use VRS. These focus groups were conducted in ASL and were videotaped. Although each focus group was scheduled for two hours, they both continued for nearly three hours.

To find participants for the focus groups, I enlisted the help of a deaf person in each state. I asked them to spread the word that I was looking for people to participate in a focus group about VRS. And I asked them to pass along my e-mail address.

Because of my distance from the site, the group in Arizona required much more hands-on assistance from the deaf person I enlisted. The person I asked to help in Arizona also coordinated all of the participants' schedules and stayed late so that I could use her office to conduct the focus group. I offered to buy each group dinner for their participation. The group in upstate New York and I went for pizza immediately after the focus group. The group in Arizona declined my offer.

Just like I did with the interviews, I had prepared a list of open-ended questions that were intended to focus on the experience of using VRS (see Appendix G). After each person introduced him- or herself to me and the group, I made a general statement: "I just want to know about your experience with VRS." From that general statement the group discussed a variety of issues ranging from text relay service to the shortage of sign language interpreters. My role in the focus group was that of a "group facilitator and moderator, managing interactions between members of the group" (Taylor and Bogdan 1998, 113). When all of the participants answered a question, I would move on to the next one. In many cases, in their responses, the participants addressed other questions I had and inspired additional ones.

Since ASL is a visual language, I used a video recorder to document the focus groups. At times, this created some unique challenges to gathering and tracking the data, as I will discuss later. As soon as I was able to, after the focus group, I would transcribe the videotapes. After I had transcribed both focus groups, I began to examine the transcriptions for themes.

My goal in coding the focus groups was to pull out the themes. I first used an open coding system. I read through the transcripts and attempted to identify the theme of a given comment. I then went back through and began to categorize comments into larger themes. I was particularly interested in themes that addressed the work deaf people had to perform while using VRS.

The coding process for the focus groups was similar to that of the interviews. However, because the number of focus group participants was far fewer than the number of interpreters I interviewed, I was able to do all of it without printing out the codes and corresponding piece of the transcripts.

Analysis of Texts

Texts have an important role in the coordination of people's everyday lives. "The text itself is to be seen as organizing a course of concerted social action" (D. Smith 1999, 121). It is often through the use of texts that practices can be coordinated and synchronized remotely. In my examination of the texts involved in VRS, I was looking for the *who* and *how* of their activation (McCoy 1995). The same text may have several purposes and those are only known once the text is taken up and activated.

> [Texts] are not made to be read as a continuous text like a novel. Rather they are read selectively for different purposes, articulated to various sequences of action, and it is these selective readings for which the text is constructed and which, in a sense, analyze it to find the sense it can make in particular settings of action. (D. Smith 2006, 68)

I learned of the texts that were significant during my participant observations, interviews, and focus groups. In some cases, I was able incorporate the texts into the interviews by asking participants about the text's function. In these cases, I asked about how the text was used and by whom.

DISTINCTIVE CONSIDERATIONS OF THIS STUDY

Every study is unique. However, when one's project involves data collection cross-culturally and cross-linguistically, those unique characteristics become more pronounced. Furthermore, because the FCC requires maintaining the confidentiality of the users of VRS, I had to be very aware of the privacy of the callers. I was also repeatedly reminded by members of the management team, as I interviewed them, of proprietary concerns they had. There are four areas in which this study was unique: ethics, politics, access, and technology.

Ethics

My first concern when embarking on this project was the ethics surrounding gathering data in a call center. I was not comfortable with the idea of watching interpreters perform their work between a deaf and non-deaf caller. I wanted to make sure that the privacy of the callers was not compromised. In addition, sign language interpreters can, at times, be skittish about their work. It has been my experience that some interpreters do not want another interpreter to observe, document, and provide analysis of their interpretation. There is a joke in the interpreting community that goes like this:

Question: How many signed language interpreters does it take to interpret the phrase, "Hi, how are you?"

Answer: Ten. One to interpret the message and nine to say how they would have done it differently.

Interpreting is very personal. Because there is no verbatim translation from ASL to English, each interpreter is providing an interpretation of how to convey a given message. Interpreting is also very competitive. Finding a flaw in one interpreter's work is one way to ensure you have more work. Because of these two factors, I had to constantly reassure interpreters that the focus of my study was not their interpretation but video relay interpreting as a new venue for service delivery.

Since I was not able to ask the callers' permission, and the FCC does not permit phone calls to be recorded, I was not going to be able to actually watch fellow interpreters perform their craft. Instead, I relied on my own experience as an interpreter working in this setting and interviews with other practitioners to begin to unfold what actually occurs in this setting.

Politics

I am not deaf. Nor I do have any person in my immediate family who is deaf. While I have been complimented by deaf people who assume I am deaf because of my fluency in their language, I believe I still retain some of my *hearing* accent when I use ASL. Just like any person who is not a native speaker, there are nuances that appear in my second language, ASL, that are residuals of my first and primary language, English.

Furthermore, Harlan Lane (1999) warns of the dangers of attempting to represent the Other. During this study, I was cognizant of the fact that I am a non-deaf person and, for at least part of my study, I would be attempting to represent deaf people and their words through my interpretation. While I am confident in my understanding of the language, and clarified any questions with the participants during the translation process, I am aware that there are power dynamics at play. As a hearing person, I was conducting research with deaf participants. Beyond my ability to hear, I was an interpreter. I was asking questions of my informants about their experiences with interpreters in VRS. I was concerned that they would see me as biased in favor of interpreters. Indeed, at times, they did ask me questions about the interpreting process and I had to phrase my responses so they were honest but also implied that I understood their rationale for how they reacted to a particular interpreter. The fact that I asked deaf people to be the initial points of contact for the groups was extremely beneficial. Even though I knew some of the participants in each focus group, they learned about this study initially from a deaf community member and, I believe, that made them more comfortable in participating.

The fact that I am not deaf has relevance beyond linguistics. In 1967, Howard S. Becker asked the thought-provoking question, "Whose side are we on?" This is a question I asked myself throughout this study. I questioned whether I was on the side of deaf people or on the side of the interpreters. Could I be on both sides? Were they different sides? Ultimately, I decided to take the standpoint (Mann and Kelley 1997) of the interpreters. My goal was to represent interpreters and the way their work was organized. However, this work included deaf people, and therefore their input was also vital.

Access

Gaining primary access to the site was not too difficult. I had been working as a sign language interpreter for ten years when I decided to take up this project and I was already providing interpreting services for Ease Communication. I had entertained the thought of a doing a covert study. I had thought since I already had access to the center in Arizona, it might be counterproductive to inform management that I was interested in researching VRS. In the end, I believe that a covert approach would have limited this study. I would not have been able to access the managers, schedulers, or directors as I did had I attempted to do a covert study.

Another way in which issues of access are relevant in the data collection for this study was the way in which information was presented. Throughout this study, I promote the idea that ASL and English are different. They are not different forms of the same language. It is due to this fact that VRS is more accessible, I argue, than text relay service. Therefore, it is ironic that I take a visual representation of deaf participant's comments and place them into an English version. I justify this decision by recognizing that first, many interested readers do not understand ASL; second, to attempt to include video clips in my work would compromise the confidentiality I guaranteed the participants. Regardless of my reasons, I recognize that the choice I have made is ableist and could potentially exclude a segment of the population I hope will find this study useful.

Technical Aspects

As I have mentioned, I chose to video record my interviews and focus groups. This allowed interpreters to switch from English to ASL without disrupting the flow of the interaction. It also allowed me to communicate with deaf people in their first language, ASL, without having to hire an interpreter to interpret into a recorder what was being said. I am not saying that one method is better than another, but for me this approach was the most acceptable. However, it did lead to some further considerations.

TRANSLATIONS

Although I am fluent in ASL, I am not a native signer. I relied on my own interpretation of the comments made during the focus groups. I am confident in my interpretation; however, because ASL and English are two different languages, it must be recognized that another bilingual individual might interpret comments slightly different. I believe that these differences would be at the lexical rather than the meaning level.

Higgins (1980) writes in his study that he chose not to record interviews with deaf people. Instead, he attempted to memorize the interviews and make his jottings at a later time, usually while he was driving away from the interview. While this was definitely an option for me, because I was doing focus groups rather than one-on-one interviews, it would have posed quite the challenge for me to remember not only what was said, but who said it. This approach would have compromised my data.

Any person who works with languages will say that context is extremely important to understanding a given message. During the focus groups, I would jot down different ideas and questions. I would also attempt to reference a particular comment that was made. Because the groups were conducted in ASL I did not use my voice. When it came time to transcribe the focus groups, it was difficult, at times, to remember which question or comment the participants were responding to. Using the jottings I made during the focus groups helped me piece together and connect comments with questions, thus providing the needed context to aid in translation.

The final technical aspect that I would like to address is the use of a video recorder to document the focus groups. Because I had no additional funding to hire someone to work the camera, I was responsible for facilitating the focus groups and controlling the camera. This was not a problem in the first focus group, as it had only two people and I merely provided the topic and allowed the participants to discuss the issue. Because they were conversing with each other, they sat in close proximity to one another and I was able to capture both on video camera without having to move the camera. The only person who was not on the video camera was me and, as I discussed earlier, that created additional challenges during the transcription process, but not during the actual focus group.

The second focus group, which consisted of four people, was larger than the first one. This meant that people were talking to each other. While it added to the depth of the information discussed, it was challenging for me to move the camera quickly enough to capture all of the comments. There were certain points when I had to ask the participants to start again.

No study is perfect. Part of the process of research is learning that understanding comes from reflecting on the process and recognizing the mistakes and complexities in the process. In this study, there were challenges, but I do not believe they compromised the data collected.

The one area that I would alter would be the video recording of the focus groups. In future studies, I believe it would be more advantageous to have another person, perhaps a research assistant, who is also fluent in ASL, to assist with the video camera. This would relieve me of having to attempt to control the video camera and facilitate the focus groups.

CONCLUSION

The approach and data collection procedures I chose were intended to yield data that would keep practitioners in view without making them the focus. The data built upon each other. I discovered whom to interview from the participant observations, and the focus groups and interviews informed which texts I examined.

Appendix B

Interpreter Certifications

NIC (NATIONAL INTERPRETER CERTIFICATION)

Individuals achieving certification at the NIC, NIC Advanced, or NIC Master level are all professionally certified interpreters. The National Interpreter Certification (NIC) exam tests interpreting skills and knowledge in three critical domains:

1. General knowledge of the field of interpreting through the NIC Knowledge exam
2. Ethical decision making through the interview portion of the NIC Performance test
3. Interpreting and transliterating skills through the performance portion of the test.

In all three domains, certificate holders must demonstrate professional knowledge and skills that meet or exceed the minimum professional standards necessary to perform in a broad range of interpretation and transliteration assignments.

NIC

Individuals who achieve the NIC level have passed the NIC Knowledge exam. They have also scored within the standard range of a professional interpreter on the interview and performance portions of the test.

NIC Advanced

Individuals who achieved the NIC Advanced level have passed the NIC Knowledge exam; scored within the standard range of a professional interpreter on the interview portion; and scored within the high range on the performance portion of the test.

NIC Master

Individuals who achieved the NIC Master level have passed the NIC Knowledge exam. They have scored within the high range of a professional interpreter on both the interview and performance portions of the test.

Individuals who achieve any of the three NIC certification levels are to be commended.

From the beginning of the test development process, under the mandate of the NAD-RID National Council on Interpreting (NCI), the subject matter experts on the test development committee were given the task of developing a test that "raised the bar" for ASL/English interpreting and transliterating standards. This resulted in the development of a challenging NAD-RID NIC test.

Passing the test at the NIC level indicates that the interpreter has demonstrated skills in interpreting that meet a standard professional performance level and should be able to perform the varied functions of interpreting on a daily basis with competence and skill. It also shows that an individual has passed a test with both interpreting and transliterating elements, as opposed to one or the other.

Additionally, with increasingly higher standards for the NIC Advanced and NIC Master levels of the test, progressively fewer individuals will meet these requirements. Achieving either the Advanced or Master level is an accomplishment and indicates that the individual exceeds the professional standards established in most routine interpreting assignments. Individuals holding the NIC Advanced and/or Master level certifications may be expected to perform competently in all routine interpreting assignments as well as in assignments that may be more complex in nature or that require interpreting skills above standard levels.

RID CERTIFICATES

CI (Certificate of Interpretation)

Holders of this certificate are recognized as fully certified in interpretation and have demonstrated the ability to interpret between American Sign Language (ASL) and spoken English for both sign-to-voice and voice-to-sign tasks. The interpreter's ability to transliterate is not considered in this certification. Holders of the CI are recommended for a broad range of interpretation assignments. **This test is available until December 2008.**

CT (Certificate of Transliteration)

Holders of this certificate are recognized as fully certified in transliteration and have demonstrated the ability to transliterate between English-based sign language and spoken English for both sign-to-voice and voice-to-sign tasks. The transliterator's ability to interpret is not considered in this certification. Holders of the CT are recommended for a broad range of transliteration assignments. **This test is available until December 2008.**

CI and CT (Certificate of Interpretation and Certificate of Transliteration)

Holders of both full certificates (as listed above) have demonstrated competence in both interpretation and transliteration. Holders of the CI and CT are recommended for a broad range of interpretation and transliteration assignments.

CDI-P (Certified Deaf Interpreter–Provisional)

Holders of this provisional certification are interpreters who are deaf or hard of hearing, and who have demonstrated a minimum of one year experience working as an interpreter; completion of at least eight hours of training on the NAD-RID Code of Professional Conduct; and eight hours of training in general interpretation as it relates to the interpreter who is deaf or hard of hearing. Holders of this certificate are recommended for a broad range of assignments where an interpreter who is deaf or hard of hearing would be beneficial. **This test is no longer available.**

CDI (Certified Deaf Interpreter)

Holders of this certification are interpreters who are deaf or hard of hearing, and who have completed at least eight hours of training on the NAD-RID Code of Professional Conduct; eight hours of training on the role and function of an interpreter who is deaf or hard of hearing; and have passed a comprehensive combination of written and performance tests. Holders of this certificate are recommended for a broad range of assignments where an interpreter who is deaf or hard of hearing would be beneficial. **This test is currently available.**

CSC (Comprehensive Skills Certificate)

Holders of this full certificate have demonstrated the ability to interpret between American Sign Language (ASL) and spoken English, and to transliterate between spoken English and an English-based sign language. Holders of this certificate are recommended for a broad range of interpreting and transliterating assignments. The CSC examination was offered until 1987. **This test is no longer available.**

MCSC (Master Comprehensive Skills Certificate)

The MCSC examination was designed with the intent of testing for a higher standard of performance than the CSC. Holders of this certificate were required to hold the CSC prior to taking this exam. Holders of this certificate are recommended for a broad range of interpreting and transliterating assignments. **This test is no longer available.**

RSC (Reverse Skills Certificate)

Holders of this full certificate have demonstrated the ability to interpret between American Sign Language (ASL) and English-based sign language or transliterate between spoken English and a signed code for English. Holders of this certificate are deaf or hard-of-hearing and interpretation/transliteration is rendered in ASL, spoken English and a signed code for English or written English. Holders of the RSC are recommended for a broad range of interpreting assignments where the use of an interpreter who is deaf or hard-of-hearing would be beneficial. **This test is no longer offered. Individuals interested in this certificate should take the CDI exam.**

OTC (Oral Transliteration Certificate)

Holders of this generalist certificate have demonstrated, using silent oral techniques and natural gestures, the ability to transliterate a spoken message from a person who hears to a person who is deaf or hard of hearing. They have also demonstrated the ability to understand and repeat the message and intent of the speech and mouth movements of the person who is deaf or hard of hearing. **This test is currently available.**

OIC:C (Oral Interpreting Certificate: Comprehensive)

Holders of this generalist certificate demonstrated both the ability to transliterate a spoken message from a person who hears to a person who is deaf or hard of hearing and the ability to understand and repeat the message and intent of the speech and mouth movements of the person who is deaf or hard of hearing. **This test is no longer offered. Individuals interested in oral certification should take the OTC exam.**

OIC:S/V (Oral Interpreting Certificate: Spoken to Visible)

Holders of this partial certificate demonstrated the ability to transliterate a spoken message from a person who hears to a person who is deaf or hard of hearing. This individual received scores on the OIC:C examination that prevented the awarding of full OIC:C certification. **This test is no longer offered. Individuals interested in oral certification should take the OTC exam.**

OIC:V/S (Oral Interpreting Certificate: Visible to Spoken)

Holders of this partial certificate demonstrated the ability to understand the speech and silent mouth movements of a person who is deaf or hard of hearing and to repeat the message for a hearing person. This individual received scores on the OIC:C examination that prevented the awarding of full OIC:C certification. **This test is no longer offered. Individuals interested in oral certification should take the OTC exam noted above.**

IC/TC (Interpretation Certificate/Transliteration Certificate)

Holders of this partial certificate demonstrated the ability to transliterate between English and a signed code for English and the ability to interpret between American Sign Language (ASL) and spoken English. This individual received scores on the CSC examination that prevented the awarding of full CSC certification. **This test is no longer offered.**

IC (Interpretation Certificate)

Holder of this partial certificate demonstrated the ability to interpret between American Sign Language (ASL) and spoken English. This individual received scores on the CSC examination that prevented the awarding of full CSC certification or partial IC/TC certification. The IC was formerly known as the Expressive Interpreting Certificate (EIC). **This test is no longer offered.**

TC (Transliteration Certificate)

Holders of this partial certificate demonstrated the ability to transliterate between spoken English and a signed code for English. This individual received scores on the CSC examination that prevented the awarding of full CSC certification or IC/TC certification. The TC was formerly known as the Expressive Transliterating Certificate (ETC). **This test is no longer offered.**

NAD CERTIFICATES

NAD III (Generalist)—Average Performance

Holders of this certificate possess above average voice-to-sign skills and good sign-to-voice skills or vice versa. This individual has demonstrated the minimum competence needed to meet generally accepted interpreter standards. Occasional words or phrases may be deleted but the expressed concept is accurate. The individual displays good control of the grammar of the second language and is generally accurate and consistent, but is not qualified for all situations.

NAD IV (Advanced)—Above Average Performance

Holders of this certificate possess excellent voice-to-sign skills and above average sign-to-voice skills or vice versa. This individual has demonstrated above average skill in any given area. Performance is consistent and accurate. Fluency is smooth, with little deleted, and the viewer has no question to the candidate's competency. With this certificate, an individual should be able to interpret in most situations.

NAD V (Master)—Superior Performance

Holders of this certificate possess superior voice-to-sign skills and excellent sign-to-voice skills. This individual has demonstrated excellent to outstanding ability in any given area. There are minimum flaws in their performance, and they have demonstrated interpreting skills necessary in almost all situations.

(Retrieved from www.rid.org on 3/28/06)

Letter Seeking Permission from VRS Provider

The Practice and Organization of Sign Language Interpreting
Jeremy L. Brunson, M.S., M.A., C.A.S. – Disability Studies, CI and CT

This research is conducted as partial requirement for the Ph.D. in sociology at Syracuse University. I am working under the direction of Professor Marjorie DeVault. Below is an overview of the study.

This study examines the work of sign language interpreters. As interpreters increase in number and visibility it is important to increase awareness of the work that interpreters do. I will conduct several in-depth interviews with various sign language interpreters, throughout the United States, about their work. I am not collecting confidential information such as clients (deaf and non-deaf) and places of employment. In the event that during interviews confidential information is divulged, all of the identifying information will be changed to pseudonyms.

As part of this study, I would like to discuss a variety of settings in which interpreters perform their work (e.g., legal, educational, community, and religious). In the last few years and with the advancement of technologies, video relay services are becoming a prominent part of the work of interpreters. As such, I would like to include a discussion about this venue of interpreting.

To do this, I would like permission to ask your staff: scheduler(s), manager(s), and director(s) at the Scottsdale, Arizona, site to allow me to interview them. I would also like permission to observe them working to better understand the role they play in your organization. Information that is considered proprietary such as call volume numbers will not be part of the study. Additionally, in accordance with the code of ethics endorsed by the Registry of Interpreters for the Deaf, I will not observe interpreters processing calls.

Thank you for taking the time to consider this research proposal. If you would like to discuss it in more depth, please feel free to contact me at 315.278.4015.

Informed Consent Form—Interviews

My name is Jeremy L. Brunson and I am a graduate student at Syracuse University. I am inviting you to participate in a research study titled "The Practice and Organization of Sign Language Interpreting: An Institutional Ethnography of Access." Involvement in the study is voluntary so you may choose to participate or not. This sheet will explain the study to you and please feel free to ask questions about the research if you have any. I will be happy to explain anything in greater detail if you wish. In addition, please feel free to contact my advisor, Professor Marjorie DeVault, at 315-443-4030, if you have any questions about this study. For information regarding the protocol I have submitted to the Institutional Review Board you may contact them at 315-443-3013. If you would like to talk to Professor DeVault or someone at the Institutional Review Board at Syracuse University, I would be happy to reimburse you for any long distance charges for the call.

I am interested in the work of sign language interpreters. As I am sure you are aware, there is a lot of literature on the mental processes that go into the production of an interpreted message. However, there has been little documentation created about those processes external to the interpreter. As such, I am interested with coming to understand how settings influence our interpreting.

You may be asked for permission to record your interview on audiotape/videotape to aid in my translation of our interview to paper. If you consent to being taped then the tape will be kept in a secure place without identifying information on it. In addition it will be disposed of after the research is complete. If you consent to being taped please sign here

_____.

If you consent to being videotaped please sign here _____.

The benefit of this research is to create a greater awareness of the work that interpreters do. I will not ask you to divulge confidential information that would be in direct conflict with the code of ethics endorsed by the Registry of Interpreters for the Deaf or policies established by Ease Communication, Inc. The risks to you of participating in this study are limited. They consist of the typical risks that are involved with sharing your thoughts, experiences, and opinions with someone. They may involve such things as the discomfort of sharing your opinion or political risk if you are to say something very critical during an interview that is overheard by someone walking by. These risks will be minimized by offering you the option to conduct an interview in a private setting and by informing the administrators of your organization that all participation in this research is to be kept confidential and I will not be able to disclose information about individual participants that may be used to identify them. Additionally, if you choose, you may assign yourself a pseudonym that will be used in all future references to your participation. I will be the only person, aside from you, who will know of the pseudonym that you have chosen. If you no longer wish to continue, you have the right to withdraw from the study, without penalty, at any time.

All of my questions have been answered and I wish to participate in this research study.

Signature of participant _____ Date _____

Print name of participant_____

Name of investigator _____ Date _____

_____

Informed Consent Form—Focus Groups

My name is Jeremy L. Brunson and I am a graduate student at Syracuse University. I am inviting you to participate in a research study titled "The Practice and Organization of Sign Language Interpreting: An Institutional Ethnography of Access." Involvement in the study is voluntary so you may choose to participate or not. This sheet will explain the study to you and please feel free to ask questions about the research if you have any. I will be happy to explain anything in greater detail if you wish. In addition, please feel free to contact my advisor, Professor Marjorie DeVault, at 315-443-4030, if you have any questions about this study. For information regarding the protocol I have submitted to the Institutional Review Board you may contact them at 315-443-3013. If you would like to talk to Professor DeVault or someone at the Institutional Review Board at Syracuse University, I would be happy to reimburse you for any long distance charges for the call.

I am interested in the work of sign language interpreters. As a deaf person you have a lot of experience in using the services of sign language interpreters. I would like to talk with you about your experiences with sign language interpreters in different settings. My goal is to have meetings with of 3 to 4 deaf people. At the end of our meeting, I will type up notes from the meeting and send them to you via email and welcome any comments.

You may be asked for permission to record your interview on audio-tape/videotape to aid in my translation of our interview to paper. If you consent to being taped then the tape will be kept in a secure place without identifying information on it. In addition it will be disposed of after the research is complete. If you consent to being taped please sign here

_____.

If you consent to being videotaped please sign here _____.

The benefit of this research is to create a greater awareness of the work that interpreters do. If you agree to participate, you and, at the most, 3 other deaf people who use sign language interpreters on a regular basis will meet and discuss your experiences. I will ask the entire group to consider a variety of questions that focus on the services of sign language interpreting and VRS. The risks to you of participating in this study are limited. They consist of the typical risks that are involved with sharing your thoughts, experiences, and opinions with someone. They may involve such things as the discomfort of sharing your opinion or political risk if you say something very critical during an interview. Because these interviews will be conducted with small groups I am unable to offer you confidentiality. However, I will ask each person to respect the privacy of others involved and not discuss who else was present. Additionally, if you choose, you may assign yourself a pseudonym that will be used in all future references to your participation. I will be the only person, aside from you, who will know of the pseudonym that you have chosen. If you no longer wish to continue, you have the right to withdraw from the study, without penalty, at any time.

All of my questions have been answered and I wish to participate in this research study.

Signature of participant _____ Date _____

Print name of participant_____

Name of investigator _____ Date _____

_____

Appendix F

Letter to Interpreters

Dear Colleague:

My name is Jeremy L. Brunson and I am a graduate student at Syracuse University. I am inviting you to participate in a research study titled "The Practice and Organization of Sign Language Interpreting: An Institutional Ethnography of Access." Some of you have already met with me during previous visits. Involvement in the study is voluntary so you may choose to participate or not. This sheet will explain the study to you and please feel free to ask questions about the research if you have any. I will be happy to explain anything in greater detail if you wish. In addition, please feel free to contact my advisor, Professor Marjorie DeVault, at 315-443-4030, if you have any questions about this study. For information regarding the protocol I have submitted to the Institutional Review Board you may contact them at 315-443-3013. If you would like to talk to Professor DeVault or someone at the Institutional Review Board at Syracuse University, I would be happy to reimburse you for any long distance charges for the call.

I am interested in the work of sign language interpreters. As I am sure you are aware, there is a lot of literature on the mental processes that go into the production of an interpreted message. However, there has been little documentation created about those processes external to the interpreter. As such, I am interested with coming to understand how settings influence our interpreting.

You may be asked for permission to record your interview on audiotape/videotape to aid in my translation of our interview to paper. If you consent to being taped then the tape will be kept in a secure place without identifying information on it. In addition it will be disposed of after the research is complete.

The benefit of this research is to create a greater awareness of the work that interpreters do. I will not ask you to divulge confidential information that would be in direct conflict with the Codes of Professional Conduct

(CPC) endorsed by the Registry of Interpreters for the Deaf or policies established by Ease Communication, Inc. The risks to you of participating in this study are limited. They consist of the typical risks that are involved with sharing your thoughts, experiences, and opinions with someone. They may involve such things as the discomfort of sharing your opinion or political risk if you are to say something very critical during an interview that is overheard by someone walking by. These risks will be minimized by offering you the option to conduct an interview in a private setting and by informing the administrators of your organization that all participation in this research is to be kept confidential and I will not be able to disclose information about individual participants that may be used to identify them. Additionally, if you choose, you may assign yourself a pseudonym that will be used in all future references to your participation. I will be the only person, aside from you, who will know of the pseudonym that you have chosen. If you no longer wish to continue, you have the right to withdraw from the study, without penalty, at any time.

If you are interested in participating in this study, or you would like more information before deciding, please feel free to contact me at jlbrunso@maxwell.syr.edu. We can also arrange a time for me to contact you via phone is that is preferable. I will be in Arizona from July 6–31, 2006. I would like to schedule interview while I am in Arizona. I am flexible as to where and when we can meet. Thank you and I look forward to hearing from you.

Sincerely,

Jeremy L. Brunson, M.S., M.A., CI and CT
Doctoral Candidate, Sociology
Syracuse University, Maxwell School of Citizenship and Public Affairs

Interview Questions

1. How did you get interested in the field of sign language interpreting?

2. Where did you get your training?
   a. How is the "real world" of interpreting different from your training?

3. How has the field of sign language interpreting changed since you began?

4. How did you get interested in doing video relay interpreting?
   a. How is video relay interpreting different from other types of interpreting?

5. What are the struggles you face doing video relay interpreting?

6. What factors went into you deciding to provide video relay interpreting?

7. What are your responsibilities here at Ease Communication, Inc.?

8. How do you negotiate issues of cultural mediation through video relay interpreting?

INTERVIEW QUESTIONS FOR STAFF WHO DO NOT PROVIDE DIRECT INTERPRETING SERVICES

1. What do you do here at Ease Communication, Inc.?

2. What is your experience with interpreting?

Focus Group Questions[31]

DEMOGRAPHIC[32]

1. Were you born deaf?
2. Are you the only person who is deaf in your family?
3. Where did you learn sign language?
4. What is your preferred means of communication?
5. When you sign, which sign system do you prefer?

FOCUS GROUP DISCUSSION POINTS

1. Tell me about your experience with video relay service.
2. In what situations do you use sign language interpreters?
3. Is there a list of interpreters you prefer?
4. What credentials do you want your interpreter to have?
5. What do you think about video relay service?
6. Tell me about the last time you used video relay service.
7. Tell me about a time when you had a really good interpreter on video relay service.
8. Tell me about a time when you had an interpreter you didn't like on video relay service.
9. Have you ever recognized an interpreter on video relay service?
   a. What do you do when you recognize the interpreter?
10. Which video relay service provider do you use the most?
   a. Why?

31. All questions will be presented in written English and American Sign Language.

32. Each person will be asked to introduce themselves including this information.

Bibliography

Abbott, Andrew. 1988. *The system of professions: An essay on the division of expert labor.* Chicago: Univ. of Chicago Press.

Bailey, Janet L. 2005. VRS: The ripple effect of supply and demand. *VIEWS* 22, no. 6: 16–17.

Baker-Shenk, Charlotte. 1991. The interpreter: Machine, advocate, or ally? In *Proceedings of the 1991 RID convention,* 120–40. Silver Spring, MD: RID Publications.

Baker-Shenk, Charlotte, and Dennis Cokely. 1980. *American Sign Language: A teacher's resource test on grammar and culture.* Washington, DC: Clerc Books.

Baldry, Chris, Phil Taylor, and Peter Bain. 2006. Bear with me . . . The problems of health and well-being in call center work. In *Institutions, production, and working life,* eds. Geoffrey Wood and Phil James, 235–54. London: Oxford Univ. Press.

Barton, Len. 1998. Sociology, disability studies, and education: Some observations. In *The disability reader: Social science perspectives,* ed. Tom Shakespeare, 53–64. London: Tower Building

Baynton, Douglas C. 1996. *Forbidden signs: American culture and the campaign against sign language.* Chicago: Univ. of Chicago Press.

Becker, Howard S. 1967. Whose side are we on? *Social Problems* 14, no. 3: 239–47.

Blanchfield, Bonnie B., et al. 2001. The severely to profoundly hearing-impaired population in the United States: Prevalence estimates and demographics. *Journal of American Academy of Audiology* 12: 183–89.

Blumer, Herbert. 1954. What is wrong with social theory? *American Sociological Review* 19, no. 1: 3–10.

Bogdan, Robert. 1988. *Freak show: Presenting human oddities for amusement and profit.* Chicago: Univ. of Chicago Press.

Braden, Jeffrey P. 1985. Interpreter professionalization: A critical review. *Journal of Interpretation* 2: 9–21.

Branson, Jan, and Don Miller. 2002. *Damned for their difference: The cultural construction of deaf people as disabled.* Washington, DC: Gallaudet Univ. Press.

Braverman, Harry. 1974. *Labour and monopoly capital: The degradation of work in the twentieth century.* New York: Monthly Review Press.

Brueggemann, Brenda Jo. 2004. Interpreting women. In *Gendering disability,* eds. Bonnie G. Smith and Beth Hutchison, 61–72. New Brunswick, NJ: Rutgers Univ. Press.

Brunson, Jeremy L. 2006. Commentary on the professional status of sign language interpreters: An alternative perspective. *Journal of Interpretation*: 2–10.

———. 2008. Your case will now be heard: Sign language interpreters as a problematic accommodation in a legal encounter. *Journal of Deaf Studies and Deaf Education* 13, no. 1: 2.

———. 2010. Visually experiencing a call: The calculated consumer labor deaf people perform to gain access through VRS. *Disability Studies Quarterly* 30, no.2. http://www.dsq-sds.org/article/view/1245/1273.

Burawoy, Michael. 1979. Manufacturing consent: Changes in the labor process under monopoly capitalism. Chicago: Univ. of Chicago Press.

Cahill, Spencer E., and Robin Eggleston. 1994. Managing emotions in public: The case of wheelchair users. *Social Psychology Quarterly* 57, no. 4: 300–312.

Campbell, Marie L. 1998. Institutional ethnography and experience as data. *Qualitative Sociology* 21, no. 1: 55–73.

———. 2008. (Dis)continuity of care: Explicating the ruling relations of home support. In *People at work: Life, power, and social inclusion in the new economy,* ed. Marjorie L. DeVault, 266–88. New York: New York Univ. Press.

Campbell, Marie L., and Fran Gregor. 2002. *Mapping social relations: A primer in institutional ethnography*. Toronto: Garamound.

Carey, Allison C. 2009. *On the margins of citizenship: Intellectual disability and civil rights in twentieth-century America*. Philadelphia: Temple Univ. Press.

Carr-Saunders, Alexander. 1928. *Professions: Their organization and place in society*. Oxford, UK: Clarendon Press.

———. 1988. Professionalization in historical perspective. In *Professionalization,* eds. Howard M. Vollmer and Donald L. Mills, 2–9. Englewood Cliffs, NJ: Prentice-Hall.

Cokely, Dennis. 1980. Sign language: Teaching, interpreting, and educational policy. In *Sign language and the deaf community: Essays in honor of William C. Stokoe,* eds. Charlotte Baker and Robbin Battison, 137–58. Silver Spring, MD: National Association of the Deaf.

———. 1992. *Interpretation: A sociolinguistic model*. Burtonsville, MD: Linstok Press.

———. 2001. Interpreting culturally rich realities: Research implications for successful interpretations. *Journal of Interpretation*: 1–45.

Collins, Patricia Hill. 1986. Learning from the outsider within: The sociological significance of black feminist thought. *Social Problems* 33: 14–32.

Conrad, Peter, and Joseph W. Schneider. 1997. Professionalization, monopoly, and the structure of medical practice. In *The sociology of health and illness* (5th ed.), ed. Peter Conrad, 163–69. New York: St. Martin's Press.

Cox, Amy. 2007. Where are your high-tech manners? *CNN.com/Technology*, July 3. http://www.cnn.com/2007/TECH/ptech/07/01/la.tech.manners/index .html (accessed on September 22, 2007).

Daniels, Arlene Kaplan. 1987. Invisible work. *Social Problems* 34, no. 5: 403–15.

Davis, Lennard J. 1995. *Enforcing normalcy: Disability, deafness, and the body.* London: Verso.

———. 2002. *Bending over backwards: Disability, dismodernism, and other difficult positions.* New York: New York Univ. Press.

Dean, Robyn K., and Robert Q. Pollard. 2001. Application of demand-control theory to sign language interpreting: Implications for stress and interpreting training. *Journal of Deaf Studies and Deaf Education* 6, no 1: 1–14.

———. 2005. Consumers and service effectiveness in interpreting work: A practice profession perspective. In *Interpreting and interpreter education: Directions for research and practice*, eds. M. Marschark, R. Peterson, and E. Winston, 259–82. New York: Oxford Univ. Press.

———. 2006. From best practice to best practice process: Shifting ethical thinking and teaching. In *A new chapter in interpreter education: Accreditation, research, and technology* (Proceedings of the 16th national convention of the Conference of Interpreter Trainers), ed. E. M. Maroney. Monmouth, OR: Conference of Interpreter Trainers.

de Montigny, Gerald A. J. 1995. The power of being professional. In *Knowledge, experience, and ruling relations: Studies in the social organization of knowledge,* eds. Marie Campbell and Ann Manicom, 209–20. Toronto: Univ. of Toronto Press.

DeVault, Marjorie L. 1991. *Feeding the family: The social organization of caring as gendered work.* Chicago: Univ. of Chicago Press.

———. 2006. What is institutional ethnography? *Social Problems* 53, no.3: 294–98.

———. 2007. Introduction. In *People at work: Life, power, and social inclusion in the new economy,* ed. Marjorie L. DeVault, 1–22. New York: New York Univ. Press.

DeVault, Marjorie L., and Liza McCoy. 2002. Institutional ethnography: Using interviews to investigate ruling relations. In *Handbook of interviewing research: Context and method*, eds. J. F. Gubrium and J. A. Holstein, 751–75. Thousand Oaks, CA: Sage Publications.

Diamond, Timothy. 1992. *Making gray gold: Narratives of nursing home care.* Chicago: Univ. of Chicago Press.

Distance Opportunities for Interpreter Training (DO IT) Center. 2005. *Video relay services interpreting task analysis report.* Greeley, CO: DO IT Center at the Univ. of Northern Colorado.

Eastwood, Lauren E. 2006. Making the institution ethnographically accessible: UN document production and the transformation of experience. In

Institutional ethnography as practice, ed Dorothy E. Smith, 181–97. New York: Rowman & Littlefield Publishers.

Emerson, Robert M., Rachel I. Fretz, and Linda L. Shaw. 1995. *Writing ethnographic fieldnotes.* Chicago: Univ. of Chicago Press.

England, Paula, and Nancy Folbre. 1999. The cost of caring. *Annals of the American Academy of Political and Social Science* 561: 39–51.

Espeland, Wendy Nelson, and Mitchel L. Stevens. 1984. Commensuration as a social process. *Annual Journal of Sociology* 24: 313–43.

Fant, Lou. 1990. *Silver threads: A personal look at the first twenty-five years of the Registry of Interpreters for the D/deaf.* Silver Spring, MD: RID Publications.

Ferri, Beth A., and David J. Connor. 2006. *Reading resistance: Discourses of exclusion in desegregation and inclusion debates.* New York: Peter Lang.

Foucault, Michel. 1972. *The archeology of knowledge and the discourse on language.* London: Tavistock.

Freidson, Eliot. 1970. *Profession of medicine: A study of the sociology of applied knowledge.* Chicago: Univ. of Chicago Press.

———. 1986. *Professional powers: A study of the institutionalization of formal knowledge.* Chicago: Univ. of Chicago Press.

———. 1994. *Professionalism reborn: Theory, prophecy, and policy.* Chicago: Univ. of Chicago Press.

Fuller, Linda, and Vicki Smith. 1996. Consumer's reports: Management by customers in a changing economy. In *Working in the service society,* eds. Cameron Lynne MacDonald and Carmen Sirianni, 74–90. Philadelphia, PA: Temple Univ. Press.

Goffman, Erving. 1961. *Asylums: Essays on the social situation of mental patients and other inmates.* Garden City, NY: Anchor Books.

———. 1963a. *Stigma: Notes on the management of spoiled identity.* Middlesex, England: Pelican Books.

———. 1963b. *Behavior in public places.* New York: Free Press.

———. 1967. *Interaction ritual: Essays on face-to-face behavior.* New York: Pantheon Books.

Goode, William J. 1957. Community within a community: The professions. *American Sociological Review* 22, no. 2: 194–200.

———. 1967. The protection of the inept. *American Sociological Review* 32, no. 1: 5–19.

Grahame, Peter R. 1998. Ethnography, institutions, and the problematic of the everyday world. *Human Studies* 21: 347–360.

Greene, Laura, and Eva Barash Dicker. 1990. *Sign me fine: Experiencing American Sign Language.* Washington, DC: Gallaudet University Press.

Greenwood, Ernest. 1957. Attributes of a profession. *Social Work* 2, no. 3: 44–55.

———. 1966. The elements of professionalization. In *Professionalization,* eds.

Howard M. Vollmer and Donald L. Mills, 9–19. Englewood Cliffs, NJ: Prentice-Hall.

———. 1988. Attributes of a profession: Revisited. In *Readings in the sociology of the professions,* eds. Sheo Kumar Lal, et al., 3–29. Delhi: Gian Publishing House.

Groce, Nora. 1985. *Everyone here spoke sign language: Hereditary deafness on Martha's Vineyard.* Cambridge, MA: Harvard Univ. Press.

Gusfield, Joseph R. 1989. Constructing the ownership of social problems: Fun and profit in the welfare state. *Social Problems* 36, no. 5: 431–41.

Hall, Edward T. 1976. *Beyond culture.* Garden City, NY: Anchor Books.

Hampton, Jean. 1999. The liberals strike back. In *Justice: Alternative political perspectives* (3rd ed.), ed. James Sterba, 249–55. Albany, NY: Wadsworth.

Haraway, Donna. 1988. Situated knowledges: The science question in feminism and the privilege of partial perspective. In *Space, gender, knowledge: Feminist readings,* eds. Linda McDowell and Joanne P. Sharp, 53–72. New York: Arnold.

Harding, Sandra. 1997. Comment on Heckman's "Truth and Method: Feminist Standpoint Theory Revisited": Whose standpoint needs the regimes of truth and reality? *Signs* 22, no. 2: 382–91.

Higgins, Paul C. 1980. *Outsiders in a hearing world: A sociology of deafness.* London: Sage Publications.

Hilder, Kay. 1995. Perceptions of the role of the American Sign Language/English interpreter. Thesis, Arizona State Univ.

Himmelweit, Susan. 1999. Caring labor. *Annals of the American Academy of Political and Social Science* 561: 27–38.

Hinrichs, Karl, William Roche, and Carmen Sirianni. 1991. From standardization to flexibility: Changes in the political economy of working time. In *Working time in transition: The political economy of working hours in industrial nations,* eds. Karl Hinrichs, William Roche, and Carment Sirianni, 3–25. Philadelphia, PA: Temple Univ. Press.

Hochschild, Arlie Russell. 1979. Emotion work, feeling rules, and social structure. *American Journal of Sociology* 85: 551–75.

———. 1983. *The managed heart: Commercialization of human feeling.* Berkeley: Univ. of California Press.

———. 1990. Ideology and emotion management: A perspective and path for future research. *Annals of the American Academy of Political and Social Science* 561: 117–42.

Hoemann, Harry W. 1986. *Introduction to American Sign Language.* Bowling Green, OH: Bowling Green Press.

Hughes, Everett C. 1960. The professions in society. *Canadian Journal of Economic and Political Sciences* 26, no. 1: 54–61.

———. 1971. Work and self. In *The sociological eye: Selected papers*, 338–47. Chicago: Aldine Atherton.

Humphrey, Janice H., and Bob J. Alcorn. 1994. *So you want to be an interpreter: An introduction to sign language interpreting*. Amarillo, TX: H & H Publishers.

Jankowski, Katherine A. 1997. *Deaf empowerment: Emergence, struggle, and rhetoric*. Washington, DC: Gallaudet Univ. Press.

Jones, Angela. 2006. Collaboration and reciprocity. *VIEWS* 23, no. 3: 6.

Kannapell, Barbara. 1982. Inside the deaf community. *Deaf American* 34, no. 4: 23–26.

Keating, Elizabeth, and Gene Mirus. 2003. American Sign Language in virtual space: Interactions between deaf users of computer-mediated video communication and the impact of technology on language practices. *Language in Society* 32: 693–714,

Kemper, Theodore D. 1990. Themes and variations in the sociology of emotions. In *Research agenda in the sociology of emotions*, ed. Theodore D. Kemper, 3–23. Albany: State Univ. of New York Press.

Kinsman, Gary. 1995. The textual practices of sexual rule: Sexual policing and gay men. In *Knowledge, experience, and ruling relations: Studies in the social organization of knowledge*, eds. Marie Campbell and Ann Manicom, 80–95. Toronto: Univ. of Toronto Press.

Kitchen, Rob. 1998. "Out of place," "knowing one's place": Space, power, and the exclusion of disabled people. *Disability and Society* 13, no. 3: 343–56.

Klein, Naomi. 2000. *No logo*. New York: Picador.

Kupritz, Virginia W. Workplace design compatibility for today's aging worker. *Journal of Industrial Teacher Education* 36, no. 3: 53–69.

Lane, Harlan. 1999. *The mask of benevolence: Disabling the deaf community*. New York: DawnSignPress.

Leidner, Robin. 1996. Rethinking questions of control: Lessons from McDonald's. In *Working in the service society*, eds. Cameron Lynne Macdonald and Carmen Sirianni, 29–49. Philadelphia, PA: Temple Univ. Press.

Leo, Richard. 1995. Trials and tribulations: Courts, ethnography, and the need for an evidentiary privilege for academic researchers. *American Sociologist* 26, no. 1: 113–34.

Lightfoot, Mary Henry. 2007. Interpreting culturally sensitive information in VRS settings. *VIEWS* 24, no. 6: 1, 17.

Linton, Simi. 1998. *Claiming disability*. New York: New York Univ. Press.

Lofland, Lyn H. 1989. Social life in the public realm: A review. *Journal of Contemporary Ethnography* 17, no. 4: 453–82.

———. 1998. *The public realm: Exploring the city's quintessential social territory*. New York: Aldine De Gruyter.

Macdonald, Cameron Lynne, and Carmen Sirianni. 1996. The service society and the changing experience of work. In *Working in the service society,* eds. Cameron Lynne Macdonald and Carmen Sirianni, 1–26. Philadelphia, PA: Temple Univ. Press.

MacDonald, Keith M. 1995. *The sociology of the professions.* Thousand Oaks, CA: Sage Publications.

Macleod-Gallinger, Janet E. 1992. The career status of deaf women: A comparative look. *American Annals of the Deaf* 137: 315–25.

Mann, Susan A., and Lori R. Kelley. 1997. Standing at the crossroads of modernist thought: Collins, Smith, and the new feminist epistemologies. *Gender and Society* 11, no. 4: 391–408.

Marx, Karl. [1867] 1976. *Capital.* Vol. I. Trans. Ben Fowkes. London, UK: Penguin.

McCoy, Liza. 2006. Keeping the institution in view: Working with interview accounts of everyday experience. In *Institutional ethnography as practice,* ed. Dorothy E. Smith, 109–25. Toronto: Rowman & Littlefield Publishers.

———. 1995. Activating the photographic text. In *Knowledge, experience, and ruling relations: Studies in the social organization of knowledge,* 181–92. Toronto: Univ. of Toronto Press.

———. 1998. Producing "What the Dean Knows." *Human Studies* 21: 395–418.

McIntosh, Peggy. 1988. *White privilege and male privilege: A personal account of coming to see correspondences through work in women's studies.* Wellesley, MA: Wellesley College Center for Research on Women.

Metzger, Melanie. 1999. *Sign language interpreting: Deconstructing the myth of neutrality.* Washington, DC: Gallaudet Univ. Press.

NAD files comments with the FCC on Video Relay Service. 2005. Retrieved November 16, 2010, from http://www.nad.org/news/2005/3/nad-files-comments-fcc-video-relay-services.

National Center for Law and Deafness. 1992. *Legal rights: The guide for deaf and hard of hearing people.* Washington, DC: Gallaudet Univ. Press.

Neumann Solow, Sharon. 2000. *Sign language interpreting: A basic resource book* (rev. ed.). Burtonsville, MD: Linstok Press.

Padden, Carol, and Tom Humphries. 1988. Deaf *in America: Voices from a culture.* Cambridge, MA: Harvard Univ. Press.

———. 2005. *Inside deaf culture.* Cambridge, MA: Harvard Univ. Press.

Pandey, Rajendra. 1988. Whither professionalism? In *Readings in the sociology of the professions,* eds. Sheo Kumar Lal et al., 63–99. Delhi: Gian Publishing House.

Patrie, Carol J. 2000. *Cognitive processing skills in English* (Effective Interpreting Series). New York: DawnSignPress.

Pernick, Martin S. 1996. *The black stork: Eugenics and the death of "defective" babies in American medicine and motion pictures since 1915.* New York: Oxford Univ. Press.

Peterson, Rico. (in press). Profession in pentimento: A narrative inquiry into interpreting in video settings. In *Moving forward in interpreting studies: Methodology and practice revisited,* ed. Laura Swabey and Brenda Nicodemus.

Quigley, Stephen P., and Joseph P. Youngs. 1965. *Interpreting for deaf people: A report of a workshop on interpreting.* Washington, DC: U.S. Government Printing Office.

Rankin, Janet M., and Marie L. Campbell. 2006. *Managing to nurse: Inside Canada's health care reform.* Toronto: Univ. of Toronto Press.

Reverby, Susan. 1997. A caring dilemma: Womanhood and nursing in historical perspective. In *The sociology of health and illness: Critical perspectives* (5th ed.), ed. Peter Conrad, 215–25. New York: St. Martin's Press.

Ritzer, George. 1996. *The McDonaldization of society* (rev. ed.). Thousand Oaks, CA: Pine Forge Press.

Rothstein, Laura. 2002. *Disability law: Cases, materials, problems* (3rd ed.). Newark, NJ: LexisNexis.

Sacks, Oliver. 1990. *Seeing voices: A journey into the world of the deaf.* New York: Vintage Books.

Schein, Jerome D. 1992. *Communication support for deaf elementary and secondary students: Perspectives of deaf students and their parents.* Edmonton: Western Canadian Centre of Studies in Deafness, University of Alberta.

Schwartz, Michael. 2006. Communication in the doctor's office: Deaf patients talk about their physicians. Ph.D. diss., Syracuse Univ.

Seal, Brenda Chafin. 2006. Fingerspelling and number literacy for educational interpreters. *VIEWS* 23, no. 3: 6–7.

Shapiro, Joseph P. 1993. *No pity: People with disabilities forging a new civil rights movement.* New York: Times Books.

Smith, Dorothy E. 1987. *The everyday world as problematic: A feminist sociology.* Boston: Northeastern Univ. Press.

———. 1990a. *Texts, facts, and femininity: Exploring the relations of ruling.* New York: Routledge.

———. 1990b. *The conceptual practices of power: A feminist sociology of knowledge.* Boston: Northeastern Univ. Press.

———. 1999. *Writing the social: Critique, theory, and investigations.* Toronto: Univ. of Toronto Press.

———. 2005. Institutional ethnography: A sociology for people. Toronto: AltaMira Press.

———. 2006. Incorporating texts into ethnographic practice. In *Institutional ethnography as practice,* ed. Dorothy E. Smith, 65–88. Toronto: Rowman & Littlefield Publishers.

Smith, George W. 1988. Policing the gay community: An inquiry into textually mediated relations. *International Journal of Sociology and the Law* 16: 163–83.

———. 1995. Accessing treatments: Managing the AIDS epidemic in Ontario. In *Knowledge, experience, and ruling relations: Studies in the social organization of knowledge,* eds. Marie Campbell and Ann Manicom, 18–34. Toronto: Univ. of Toronto Press.

Spector, Malcolm, and John I. Kitsuse. 2001. *Constructing social problems.* New Brunswick, NJ: Transaction Publishers.

Starr, Paul. 1982. *The social transformation of American medicine: The rise of a sovereign profession and the making of a vast industry.* New York: Basic Books.

Steinberg, Ronnie J., and Deborah M. Figart. 1999. Emotional labor since *The managed heart. Annals of the American Academy of Political and Social Science* 561: 9–26.

Stewart, David A., Jerome D. Schein, and Brenda E. Cartwright. 1998. *Sign language interpreting: Exploring its art and science.* Boston: Allyn and Bacon.

Taylor, Marty M. 1993. *Interpretation skills: English to American Sign Language.* Edmonton, Alberta: Interpreting Consolidated.

———. 2002. *Interpretation skills: American Sign Language to English.* Edmonton, Alberta: Interpreting Consolidated.

Taylor, Phil, and Peter Bain. 1999. "An assembly line in the head": Work and employee relations in the call centre. *Industrial Relations Journal* 30, no. 2: 101–17.

Taylor, Steven J., and Robert Bogdan. 1998. *Introduction to qualitative research methods: A guidebook and resource (*3rd ed.). New York: John Wiley & Sons.

Tipton, Carol. 2006. Unique challenges of interpreting from ASL to English. *VIEWS* 23, no. 2.

Tucker, Bonnie. 1997. The ADA and deaf culture: Contrasting precepts, conflicting results. *Annals of the American Academy of Political and Social Science* 549 (1): 24–36.

van den Broek, Diane. 2004. "We have the values": Customers, control, and corporate ideology in call centre operations. *New Technology, Work and Employment* 19, no. 1: 2–13.

Weisenberg, Julia C. 2007. From telephone to dial tone: A look at video interpreting. *VIEWS* 24, no. 6.

Wertz, Richard W., and Dorothy C. Wertz. 1997. Notes on the decline of midwives and the rise of medical obstetricians. In *The sociology of health and illness: Critical perspectives* (5th ed.), ed. Peter Conrad, 170–82. New York: St. Martin's Press.

Wilensky, Harold L. 1964. The professionalization of everyone? *American Journal of Sociology* 70, no. 2: 137–58.

Williams, Gareth. 1998. The sociology of disability: Towards a materialist phenomenology. In *The disability reader: Social science perspectives,* ed. Tom Shakespeare, 234–44. London: Tower Building.

Winefield, Richard. 1999. *Never the twain shall meet: The communication debate.* Washington, DC: Gallaudet Univ. Press.

Witter-Merithew, Anna, and Leilani J. Johnson. 2005. *Toward competent practice: Conversations with stakeholders.* Alexandria, VA: Registry of Interpreters for the Deaf.

Index

occupations, professions compared to, 7
"off call" state, 122–23, 124, 128
"on call" state, 122–23
organizational complex, 28
organization of practices, 109–11. *See also* texts

participant observation, 159–61
pay for interpreters
    incentive pay, 48
    increases in, 146
    interpreters-in-training and, 38
    as motivation to work for VRS, 85–86
    types of interpreting and, 12
peak hours, problems of, 78
people of color, interpreting for, 95–96
perceptions, influence of, 91
Point of Contact duty, 54
power
    dynamics of, 167–68
    over callers, exercise of, 94, 99–101
    of professions, 7–9
problematics, 26, 155
productivity reports
    Activity Log, 123–25, 128–29
    Minutes Generated Report, 123, 127–28
    Productivity Report, 123, 125–30
products, 26–28
professionalization of sign language interpreting, ix, 6–11
Professional Powers (Freidson), 7–8, 9–10
proletariatization of professions, 9–10, 11
providers of VRS
    fraudulent calls and, 139–41
    letter seeking permission from, 177
    lobbying by, 148
    as for-profit organizations, 113–14
    revenue of, 131
    at RID conference, 150
    rules and regulations of, 148–49
    See also Ease Communication, Inc.

public lives of deaf people, 66–68

quality, measures of, 119–22, 135

rates of reimbursement, 127, 130, 131–32
receiving calls
    billable time, 55–56
    call setup, 55
    identity and, 57–60
    returning calls to queue, 61–62
    types of calls, 56–57
receptive work, opportunities to practice, 86–88
Registry of Interpreters for the Deaf (RID)
    certification by, ix, 85, 172–76
    codes of conduct of, 94–95
    establishment of, 5
    role of, 5–6
    Standard Practice Paper on Video Interpreting, 111–12
    VRS providers and, 148, 150
regulation
    of professionals, 8
    of text relay services, 69–71
    See also FCC
reimbursement for VRS, 127, 130–34
relationships
    changes to, 143–45
    between interpreters and deaf people, 3
repetitive strain injury, 32–33, 37, 132
reports. *See* productivity reports
research, purpose of, 144–45
returning calls to queue, 61–62
RID. *See* Registry of Interpreters for the Deaf
ruling relations, 111, 135, 137

schedulers, 39–41, 157
scheduling process for VRS centers, 48–53
scripts, for non-deaf people, 59–60
semilinguals, 16
seniority and work schedules, 39–41

service providers, 79–80. *See also* Ease
  Communication, Inc.; providers
  of VRS; sign language interpreters
shared work spaces, 45–46
shifts, ending, 62–63
sign language interpreters
  asking for another, or reporting, 77
  availability of, 122–23
  certification of, ix, 85, 171–76
  as cultural bridges, 83–84
  deaf people and, 3, 94–95
  employment of, 12, 150
  impact of VRS work on, 146–48
  as informants, 157
  letter to, 182–83
  managers as, 41–42
  qualified, definition of, 82
  qualified, lack of, 75–77, 81, 98–99
  standpoint of, 168
  as transparent, 57–58
  in VRS centers, 35–39
sign language interpreting
  access and, 1
  anxiety and, 86, 87
  definition of, 82
  emotional labor in, 99–105
  employment and salary for, 11–12
  exemption from provision of, 146
  field of, 5–6
  fluency in, 65
  making work of visible, 117–19
  misunderstandings and, 70–71,
    72–74, 145–46
  models of, 12–15
  multiple demands of, 105–6
  professionalization of, ix, 6–11
  work of, 83–84
  written ASL and, 70–71
  See also American Sign Language
sites of data collection, 157–59
skills enhancement, opportunities for,
  86–88
Smith, Dorothy
  influence of, 26, 164
  on institutional ethnography, 153
  on institutions, 24, 109

  on ruling relations, 141
  on work knowledge, 82
sociology
  of interpreting, 137–41
  of work and professions, 141–42,
    143
"speed of answer" measurement,
  50–51, 123
staff interpreters, 35–36
standardization of practices
  creation of, 114–17
  documents and, 32
  interactive service work and, 105
supervision component of
  professional practice, 149

teaming, 124
technical support staff of centers, 43
technological interface at VRS centers
  call distribution, 46–48
  Instant Messaging, 53–54
  scheduling, 48–53
technology
  computer-mediated communication
    and, 146–47
  data collection and, 169–70
  dependence on, 143
Telecommunication Device for the
  Deaf. *See* teletypewriter
Telecommunication Enhancement Act,
  31
telecommunication relay services, 20,
  21
telephone companies, Title IV of ADA
  and, 19, 20
telephone services
  access via, 67–68
  calculated consumer labor of using,
    75–79
  evolution of, 19–22
  of non-deaf people, 108–9
  uses of, 30–31
teletypewriter (TTY), 20, 21, 69
text relay services
  effectiveness of, 16–17
  establishment of, 68–69